THE  RALLY TEAM
IN AUSTRALIA

BOOK ONE: 1974-1981

BY DEREK RAWSON
WITH CONTRIBUTIONS FROM FELLOW TEAM MEMBERS

First published as Print on Demand paperback by IngramSpark April 2021
Revision one, May 2021
Revision two, June 2021
Revision three, July 2022
Rivision four, March 2025

Text © Derek Rawson 2020

ISBN: 978-0-6451661-0-1

Copyright is claimed for this book as a whole. Please feel free however to quote or use sections of text for your own purposes. Creating this book has been more a labour of love than a money making exercise, its purpose to share some memories of these 'Golden Years', both with those who helped make them and also with those who've come along since. I've also wanted to offer more complete characterisations of some of the actors in this story as some have been deified through repeated telling of various stories, particularly in recent years via social media, and a record should always be set straight.

Please feel free to offer corrections or additions if you feel you have contradicting or additional information that you think should be disclosed or corrected.

The photos used herein (many of which are rather dodgy but I thought important) are from a large collection I've amassed from many sources over 40+ years and I regret I've not kept most of the source information with the photos. If you wish to claim ownership of a selected image or images, please contact me. I will be more than happy to add source acknowledgements to subsequent printings or to remove and replace images if required.

Please contact me via email: djr@pobox.com

A catalogue record for this book is available from the National Library of Australia

Cover images
Top panel from left:
    Dunkerton/Beaumont 1976 Marchal Rallye, LHD 240Z
    Fury/Suffern 1976 Southern Cross Rally, 710
    Dunkerton/Beaumont 1978 Rally of the West, 710
    Fury/Suffern 1978 Marchal Rallye, Stanza
    Dunkerton/Beaumont 1980 Bega Valley Ralley, Stanza
Bottom: Team photo taken in Perth 1980.
From left, Monty Suffern, George Fury, Derek Rawson, George Smith,
    Howard Marsden, Peter Ryan, Jamie Drummond, Jeff Beaumont, Ross Dunkerton.

"Following the successful debut of the Datsun Racing Team in 1966, it was decided to form a Datsun Rally Team with well-known rally driver Bruce Wilkinson as manager. It will be recalled that Wilkinson had been a member of the Datsun team that won its class in the 1958 Mobilgas Trial."

— Introducing Datsun to Australia by G.R. Denner

Rallies could certainly pull a crowd back in the 1970s. Here is the finish of the 1974 Southern Cross Rally in Sydney. George Fury's 4th O/R and class winning 180B SSS can be seen at left in the foreground.

CONTENTS

Acknowledgements .... 1 & 203
Team Members 3
Southern Cross Drivers 35
and Navigators 38
The Story
    Precis 39
    Early Days 43
    1973 53
    1974 58
    1975 62
    1976 71
    1977 84
    1978 95
    1979 117
    1980 130
    1981 144
Cars
    610 SSS 155
    240Z 157
    710 SSS 159
    Stanza 167
    Sunny 181
    Patrol Desert Racer 183
    620 Rally Ute 184
    E20 Vans 185
Engines
    LR 189
    LZ 190
    L20B 193
    Thanks for all the help 194
Addendums
    Early Datsun rally successes 195
    Datsun/Nissan model nomenclature 200

ABOUT THE AUTHOR

After a five-year merchandising cadetship with Repco (Replacement Parts Pty Ltd in those days) which included a string of postings in several branches, the advertising section, the marketing department, the sales counter in their head office showroom, the reception counter in their engineering section, and also a RMIT Preliminary Motor Mechanics course, I found myself as a travelling sales rep in a minor Repco branch, and hated it. I left and went to work in Stillwell Ford's parts counter and hated that even more.

In the first of a series of fortuitous events in 1973 my girlfriend's father, who was the Used Car Manager of the Datsun Sales Centre, offered me a job as a Service Receptionist/Advisor in the Datsun Service Centre with whom the Used Car division shared premises. There I was to discover that a good number of the company's management were into rallying, and I was soon hooked. In 1974 I was enlisted to help prepare the works rally cars of an evening at Bruce Wilkinson Motors in the lead-up to the Southern Cross Rally and for 1975 I also got a gig on the Datsun service crew for the 'Cross'.

When our Service Centre moved to larger premises in South Melbourne at the end of 1975, I was to find we shared those premises with an executive wing of the Clayton Manufacturing division, headed by Mr Hisashi Sasamoto, NMA's Chief Engineer, Vice President, and No. 1 rally fan. After a string of rotten luck and poor results at the Southern Cross International, Nissan (probably Sasamoto) decided the rally team should be brought inside the company and 'done' at a more professional level and I guess, as he was aware he already had a rally service mechanic on-site, decided I should take it on full-time. Only a few short weeks later I met the delightful Howard Marsden – newly recruited Rally Team Manager.

By late 1977 as the team had grown, I'd gravitated to, and taken responsibility for, the engines and this was to be my lot in the team through to its re-privatisation, and my moving on in 1985.

ACKNOWLEGEMENTS

Firstly I'd like to acknowledge and thank Howard Marsden who, from 1976, led our newly corporatised motor sport team for the nine years we rallied and then raced for Nissan Motor Co., until the team was privatised once again in 1985. He kept faith in me as I continued to grow into my role. I wish he were still with us.

Secondly, the heroes who made all our long hours and efforts worthwhile, most of all: George Fury, Monty Suffern, Ross Dunkerton, Jeff Beaumont, Geoff Portman (dec), Ross Runnalls and Bill Evans. But also the international Southern Cross drivers and navigators who will all get a mention shortly.

Thirdly, our inner circle of heroic teammates with whom I shared six close and adventurous years of rallying and four of whom went on to also share the four years of circuit racing. Listed here in the chronological order they arrived on my Datsun stage.

1974	Bruce Wilkinson
1976	Howard Marsden (dec)
	Bill Evans
	Barry Nelson
	Jamie Drummond (dec)
1977	Peter Davis
1978	Peter Ryan
1979	Peter Anderson
1980	George Smith

There were several Japanese mechanics who showed up repeatedly for Southern Cross rallies through those years, some of those also turned up for the 1981 and '82 James Hardie 1000s at Bathurst.

Sas, here with Wakabayashi (left) and Marsden (right) on the '77 Southern Cross

For me though, the most significant Japanese, although resident in Australia and not part of the team per se, was **Mr Hisashi Sasamoto**, for without him, my adventure would likely have never begun.

Richard Power (of NMA Marketing and who you'll hear more from) says of him: *"A key senior figure in NMA was chief engineer Hisashi 'Sas' Sasamoto, who showed measured interest in the factory team in his own, somewhat mysteriously muted way.*

"Mostly serious, he did have a flicker of impish humour and used to start many sentences in his 'Japanenglish' with the word 'whether', completely out of context. To this day, after decades of incommunicado, when I now chat with Wilko, our conversation is still comically, illogically, laced with this word."

My own experience of Sas was that he demonstrated fanatical although reserved interest in the factory team and, especially in my early years, was always there when we were campaigning. But gregarious he certainly was not, my guess is that he was rather self-conscious about his limited command of English and preferred to remain in the background in our presence. Always ready in white work gloves to lend a hand, although I never witnessed it, I'm sure he'd have slid under a car if the need arose.

The Japanese crew members who repeatedly showed up in Australia for the Southern Cross International and then also for the first couple of years of the James Hardie 1000 after we transitioned to racing, were:

Wakabayashi san
Intern'l Team Manager

Mabo Kobayashi
Head Mechanic

Gun Kobayashi
Head Mechanic

Shinoda san
Team Manager

Heichan Kato
Engine Man

Saito san
Mechanic

Iio san
Dunlop Tyre techn'n

Several people helped mightily with the preparation of this manuscript and I will acknowledge them in conclusion.

Core TEAM MEMBERS
in order of their appearance on my Datsun rally stage.

BRUCE WILKINSON

Bruce is a terrific Aussie bloke. Back in the day he had the Datsun Dealership on the corner of Toorak and Summerhill Rds Hartwell (just west of the railway overpass of Toorak Road) and approx 13kms east of Melbourne, and he captained the Datsun Rally Team from there for about 10 years. It's apartments now of course.

I first met Bruce in 1974 and I'm still in occasional contact with him. He seems to have changed so little since that day.

Richard and Bruce – 1973

Richard Power, at the time working in Nissan Motor Co (Aust)'s Marketing Department, was involved with the Rally Team under Bruce Wilkinson before I arrived on the scene so I'll let Richard describe Bruce for you in his most eloquent style:

"Bruce is a selfless, generous, methodical and gnomish character who cultivated deep ties with key Nissan people in Japan from his small Datsun dealership in Hartwell. He used to mightily amuse senior NMC rally people at airport pickups in his 1950s Rolls Royce Silver Cloud saloon.

Affectionately dubbed 'Wide Part' by some, Wilko was a long term rallyist who had competed successfully back in the 1958, 16,250km Mobilgas Round Australia Trial, co-driving/navigating with a pair of Japanese drivers in an early Datsun 210 1000 entered by the factory in Japan. In winning their class, they registered Nissan's first motorsport victory anywhere in the world.

Wilko had great endurance and could survive on almost no sleep, a big asset as a team boss and hands-on service crew leader in those dangerous days of long endurance trials and multi-night rallies.

As an aside, he quotes NMC rally team bosses, who later came to Australia as part of the Southern Cross Rallies from 1972, commenting that his operation was the only one around all Nissan's global rally presences where they could rely on special rally parts and tools not disappearing locally between their annual visits."

MONTY SUFFERN

Something of a boffin, Monty worked as a lecturer in Chemical Engineering at Swinburne Technical College (these days Swinburne University of Technology) in Hawthorn, Victoria where, in the late 1960s, he met George Fury, working at the time as a lab technician. George had been inspired while spectating on the '68 London to Sydney Marathon and was keen to have a go. Having worked alongside Monty for a number of years, and feeling that he was halfway intelligent, George asked whether Monty was up for the challenge and they teamed up, becoming one of the most successful and longest enduring partnerships in rallying in Australia.

Monty says: *"The learning curve was steep, and in our very first event (in George's early model Ford Cortina) we were blindingly fast, but had a road card where many of the control officials marked 'WD' against our early arrival time. We figured that must have meant "Well Done" and were rather surprised at the mammoth score we accumulated by the end. We soon got the hang of it though, and our first win in the Cortina was the 1973 Akademos Rally."*

Monty was to have teamed with Gil Davis in a works-assisted 180B SSS for the 1973 Southern Cross Rally, but when Gil had to withdraw from the event, he insisted that the navigator position offered to Monty be honoured, and in turn Monty suggested to Team Manager Wilkinson, that George would make a good substitute driver. George immediately took three weeks annual leave from Swinburne to help prepare the car. And so it was – they showed they had what it took to be a formidable crew and the rest is history (mostly contained in these pages ☺)

Monty tells that early in their partnership there were doubts about his abilities: *"George did run an event with Roger Bonhomme while Bruce Wilkinson was managing the team, to see if they could figure out why I was making the occasional blunder. I think they found out that everyone makes the odd mistake and George remained faithful to me, for which I was immensely grateful. The other event I recall was in Western Australia when George ran with John Large for one event, and was unimpressed – he did not particularly relate* to John's style of egging him along – a bit like Freddie Gocentas who used to thump the windscreen, screaming go, go, go. I think the quiet refined approach like mine was more Geo's style. Anyway, the history books are on my side."

Monty has a rather cheeky smile and he proved to be a most popular, valuable and very welcome part of our team, not only as a competent and complementary, in-car teammate for George, but also as an expert technical consultant for any number of issues with materials, lubricants, adhesives and the like, which contribute to building and running a competition vehicle at a high level. Together with an electronics boffin colleague, John Bailey, Monty collaborated on the building of an electronic rally computer and distance display to replace the cable-driven, analog device of the day, the Halda. 'Monty's Black Box' endured through at least two versions and went on to gain notoriety and fame and become part of the mystique and fascination of the 'Golden Era' of rallying in Australia. See photo page 114

Monty says: "John was a friend of a Monash Uni colleague of mine who introduced us. As you say, lovely bloke, and we hit it off right away. Result was, he and Andy (the Monash guy) came up to Mount Slide one night when we were testing and I think George took them for a ride. John said "I think I could make some electronic device to replace the Halda" and after a couple of evenings meeting with him, out popped Black Box version 1. An emerging technology had John thinking that he could improve on the concepts, resulting in Black Box 2. The detail he went to was amazing, including: "do you want this parameter to start (or zero) when you press the button, or when you let it go?"

Monty was equal Australian Rally Champion Navigator in 1977 and Champion Navigator in his own right in 1980. Together as always with George, he won the Southern Cross International Rally in 1978 and '79.

These days Monty and wife Suzi live in Texas in the U.S.A. where they went for a teaching opportunity in late 1999.

Monty is also a very talented Rag-Time Jazz pianist – search for 'Monty Suffern piano' and be entertained by the Piano Guy on YouTube!

In case you think that's not enough for one life, Monty has also built and flown his own aircraft, the 2016 MONTY SUFFERN VELOCITY XL-FG fixed-wing, 4 seater, with a single 260 bhp 4-cyl engine. Not too dissimilar to the old Stanza engine really ☺.

GEORGE FURY

Six years older than me and with an already impressive record of rallying success, George arrived in my life a ready-made hero. From 1973 when I watched him in my first Southern Cross Rally and especially after he took me for a ride in the 710 at Mt Slide (near Toolangi, north east of Melbourne where we used to test) in 1976, he became a figure of awe which was enhanced somewhat by his slight aloofness – a factor of his  characteristic shyness. He was to be a key character in my life for the following 10 years.

A talented, practical engineer, great thinker, laser focussed and naturally gifted driver, he'd have been at the top of any rally team manager's wish list. Thanks are due to Bruce Wilkinson who recognised his talent and gave him the break he needed to burst onto the National rally scene and quickly lock-in his place. George became part of the package requisitioned by Nissan Australia late in 1975.

He came to the team fully optioned with navigator Monty, and lovely girlfriend Margie Bronner. Margie had a house in Hawthorn that she vacated to move to the Talmalmo farm that was to become their home on the Murray River for the next 45+ years. This allowed me to raise my hand as a prospective tenant for her Hawthorn house and it became my abode for a couple of years until I bought my own place.

Born in Hungary on January 31, 1945, George came to Australia with his family at age 13 and grew up on the family farm, arguably one of the best places to develop practical engineering skills. He was inspired by the cars in the 1968 London to Sydney Marathon flashing by on dirt roads and had to give it a try for himself. It must have been gratifying to discover he had a natural flair.

Working at Melbourne's Swinburne Technical College (these days Swinburne University of Technology) as a lab technician, he befriended lecturer, Monty Suffern and they decided, in 1972, to have a go at a rally in George's Mk1 Cortina. Success was almost immediate as they won the Melbourne University Car Club's Akademos Rally in East Gippsland early in '73 (beating Gil Davis in one of the works 180B SSSs) and were soon after offered the opportunity to take over the 180B SSS Gil Davis had begun building with the assistance of Bruce Wilkinson, for the '73 Southern Cross Rally. George immediately took several weeks off work and threw himself into the project. He and Monty were entered by Nissan Motor Co. (Aust) as Car 35. They retired early in Div. 2 with a blown motor but had shown their potential.

A strong fifth in the Don Capasco Rally early in '74 with that car, led to George and Monty being offered the green works 180B SSS for the '74 Cross – the car Frank Kilfoyle had used in the '73 event. This turned out to be the toughest Cross to that date and since, with only ten cars left to start Div. 4. Only 'the magnificent seven' survived to see the finish. Fury and Suffern, Car #18, had a mortgage on third place till late in the event and had to settle for fourth following Cowan and Singh in their mighty works Mitsubishi Lancers and a Japanese privateer in a Toyota Trueno. It was their performance in this event where George and Monty really cemented their places in the Datsun Rally Team.

They trained and worked diligently and determinedly as a team at all aspects of the sport – they could change a flat in under two minutes in a choreographed sequence of tasks which remain secret to this day. Part of the secret though, was to have the wheel brace affixed to the floor just in front of Monty's seat. Monty says, *"This location provided for additional 'fun' when George would ask to 'borrow' it to remove the nut retaining the steering wheel so he could shift it around a spline or two to straighten the steering on the odd occasion when they'd hit a rock or some such. The exciting part of this was that this was done at 80 to 100 kph, although you'll be pleased to know, most often on transport sections."*

George was highly skilled, very fast, tenacious, mechanically sympathetic, fit and tough, and he knew how to get the best from his car and his support team – we *really* wanted to help him win. He was also an excellent development driver, able to give Howard and our crew clear feedback when testing. He was, more often than not, thoughtful. While Dunko was clowning around, George might be seen sitting with his notebook in contemplation of some mechanical challenge. I once awoke during a night in a motel room I was sharing with George somewhere and he was sitting up in bed with that serious expression and scribbling away in his always handy notebook. Funny, some of the things you remember.

He was also quite shy and self conscious which seemed rather at odds with his fierce determination to win, so that, when he did, he was never very comfortable on the podium or on the stage receiving his trophy. He had an endearing smile but often seemed afraid to show it. I'm guessing he was self conscious about thinning hair, as from mid to later years with the team he would only ever be seen in helmet or the red terry-towelling hat. He seemed to shun the limelight and seemed happier to be one of the boys than having to pander to the media, the sponsors, or even the other crews, he was our hero and he appeared to enjoy being amongst us. How good.

George, almost always with Monty navigating, had a hugely impressive record of successes with the Datsun Rally Team. In the period 1973–1981, he had 13 top level rally wins for Datsun in Australia (Australian Championship or international events), seven second places, and two thirds. In that same period George won two Australian Championships (one shared with teammate Dunko), two gruelling Southern Cross rallies and a Castrol International. He went from complete novice to Australian Champion Driver in just three years, and to winner of our most prestigious and highest level event, the Southern Cross International, in four.

George proved to be an extraordinary testing and development driver and should take credit for much of the thinking that went into our cars' advances between 1977 and 1985.

He had a total of 12 DNFs in the rallying years, 8 of which were mechanical failures, more often than not when leading. Many of these mechanical failures were engine related and several of those, breakages of one of the camshafts' drive gears on the LZ DOHC engine we used between 1976 and 1981. It should be noted we were pushing the hardware very hard in order to compete with the BDG-powered Ford Escorts of the day – custom built sports sedans in comparison with our 710 Violets and the 160J Stanzas. If George and Monty had had more reliable hardware under them, their record would have been even more impressive.

Richard Power says of George: *"George was mostly a quiet, smiley, somewhat unflappable yet steely impatient hyper speedster on any surface, rally or race. A mechanical engineer-cum-farmer who, pre-Datsun, built his own highly effective rally Mk 1 Cortina with a 2-litre engine transplant when most other amateurs had migrated to Datsun 1600s, George could drive at the max but still with meccanico simpatico to preserve the car."*

HOWARD MARSDEN

Whereas Bruce Wilkinson was a great Aussie bloke, his replacement, Howard Marsden was a true English gentleman. Was this a good thing? Well, the answer is a resounding Yes, and No. His modus operandi was to tell people what he thought they wanted to hear, in a very friendly and never condescending manner. He would keep this up until he'd backed himself into a corner and then, when it all broke down, he could be quite blunt. I'm quite sure many of those who had dealings with him would have preferred to skip the preliminaries and get straight to blunt. Working under Howard could be very frustrating until we finally accepted we couldn't depend on him doing what he said he'd do, and then, late in the day, we learned to work around that.

That said though, we were truly blessed to be captained by Howard – I shudder to contemplate how different an experience it would have been had Harry Firth accepted that role – which was first offered to him.

Howard's contract with Nissan came with the senior executive position of Product Evaluation Manager and he had a nice office and secretary (mercifully) in Nissan Australia's head office on Frankston-Dandenong Road, South Dandenong. As he was quoted in the media, *"Datsun is the only company which has a direct link from our motorsport program back into the company."* Also though, *"My motorsport activities are a relatively small part of my job".*

I struggle to reconcile the vision of Howard sitting in that office with my memory of him seated in the backwards-facing, removable seat in Jamie's van while we hurtled along country roads chasing after rally cars!

His executive role must have kept him pretty busy (he had several work trips to Japan for instance) so that apart from when we were away on events or out testing, neither of which he ever missed, we saw little of him. I estimate that on average he'd pay us a visit at the workshop something less than once per fortnight and usually not stay very long.

Howard was a complex being. Darling to the motoring media and our team's many fans, he could be a major frustration to those he worked for and to those of us who depended upon him for guidance. It's really not my intention to sully his memory but there are a few stories that we laugh uproariously over when we get together these days, and I hope he'd not mind too much my sharing a couple here after his passing. While alive I think he'd likely have have been pretty embarrassed but I take solace in the knowledge that death saves us from these human frailties.

Part of telling people what he thought they wanted to hear involved making promises, some of which I struggle to accept he truly believed he could deliver. And yet I wonder now whether he had a faith that whatever it was would become real if he put it out there. Some of these not-quite-manifested promises had quite extreme consequences, such as when up-and-coming rally hot-shot, Bob Nicoli, towed his 4-wheel trailer across from Perth and arrived at our Braeside, Melbourne workshop to collect the rally Stanza Howard had promised him. For a hot-shot rally driver, Bob in those days was a pretty laconic and laid-back character, the news that we knew nothing about any Stanza for him, that there wasn't a rally car available, and that Howard was away on holidays, was greeted with, at first confusion, then disbelief, and then only philosophical acceptance followed by his turning around and heading back across our vast country. I don't even remember him smoking his tyres out our gate! Oh to be blessed with the ability to summon so much calm.

There were many times over the years that we the 'hands on' got to a stage of needing guidance and decisions made, and we'd request a face-to-face. He'd schedule a meeting at his office and, at the appropriate time, we'd get cleaned up and drive up there only to find HM was not there and his secretary had no idea where he was. We'd wait a while and then head back to work. On occasions when he'd turn up at the workshop, we'd all sit down with a coffee (or tea of course in his case). We'd spend a half hour or more together and we'd feel heard, appeased and even satisfied but, on getting back to the problems at hand, realise we'd received no relevant decisions and few relevant pearls of wisdom. Howard was master at this. He seemed to have complete faith that passionate and dedicated people would make good choices and work their way through any problem that arose – and we usually did.

On one occasion we had his Skyline at the workshop for some work (fitting the giant pump-up antenna or something) and one of us discovered a cheque on the rear floor, dirty footprints and all. It was for $10,000, from Total Oil, made out to Nissan Motor Co., and dated some months prior. Knowing it would be an embarrassment if we drew his attention to it, we left it where we found it. And there it stayed for months longer. We always had a big laugh when one of us noticed it hadn't moved when next we saw the car. Total must have rung eventually to say hey, you know last year's sponsorship cheque…

Under Harry Firth, development would likely have proceeded at a faster rate, but we workers would not have had to think and problem solve, we'd not have been empowered. I can now thank Howard's memory for this great gift and wish I'd done so as we were parting ways. At the time though, I was too embroiled in the frustration.

On events though, Howard was utterly brilliant. On the Southern Cross Internationals of 1978, '79 and '80 which we won with Stanzas, he had a fairly large team to manage and co-ordinate. We service crews, got by with little sleep over the four days of the event. Howard though, got even less, as each morning, before we jumped in the vans to head out, we were each handed a comprehensive set of instructions and maps covering the mountainous terrain being used for the coming division. On these were marked the competitor's route and the suggested route for us to access our assigned stage ends throughout the forests. Howard and Rex Muldoon, or later, Howard and Phil Rainer, would have been up earlier, after going to bed later, to plan the following night's service activities – and it all worked, almost without a hitch.

Howard and Rex/Phil would head out into the forests in the 2-door orange Skyline with its enormous pump-up VHF aerial mounted astern. They'd hunt out the highest accessible spots to create useable radio comms for the territory in use that night, in order to be able to direct and resolve issues arising. We all took pride in this endeavour and its success.

When we needed to be focused on the cars, HM was always on hand to distract and sweet-talk the ever-present journos. Thank you Howard. I don't know how but I think you actually enjoyed this role. It was always amusing to see what turned up in Auto Action a week or so later.

Howard's serious and professional nature was a good match for lead driver George Fury and they enjoyed an enduring and successful relationship. Navigator Monty Suffern's quiet and methodical nature also fitted right in. The success the team enjoyed was due in no small part to this great 3-way partnership. The relationship that simmered just below the surface between Howard and the flamboyant, raucous, indefatigable and tenacious Ross Dunkerton was another thing altogether. I'm sure Howard found his philandering and irreverent ways an embarrassment and would have preferred to have had nothing to do with him, but the alternative – to be competing against him – was just too daunting a prospect. I'm so grateful they managed to endure each other because Ross, and like-minded co-driver Jeff Beaumont, added mightily to both our success record and to building the legend and mystique of the Datsun Rally Team.

Another episode that illustrates Howard's 'management style' centres on our post rally celebrations after a successful Australian Rally Championship event in Western Australia. We were staying in a very nice, 4 or 5-story hotel in a suburb of Perth and they had some waste-high earthenware pots in the lift foyers. After a few too many beers downed by aforementioned service crew, it seemed like a humorous idea to put these pots in the lift and send them down to reception. First one then four or five. There was much hilarity.

After returning to Melbourne (and that's another good yarn I'll save for later), at a debriefing meeting at our workshop, Howard produced a bill from the hotel for the replacement of one 3 foot earthenware vase. "Do you boys know anything about this?" Four blank guileless faces were our response. "OK, well I'll just mark this to be paid," was his knowing reply. Things needed to be far more serious before he'd be willing to confront. We did hear several times in following years though, that "You boys are becoming very expensive."

A couple of years later, we were testing at Calder Raceway and had some visiting Japanese in attendance. Jamie was standing at the front of the early Bluebird racer, while at the rear, Howard was regaling the Japanese with his prodigious engineering skills. In response to an unheard question, Howard said it had been he who'd designed the modifications to the rear suspension. Poor Jamie came as close as he ever had to the top of his head coming off – I swear we could see steam coming out of his ears. Had HM been asked about this later (and there's a good possibility he was as Jamie's wrath did not subside quickly), Howard would have had a good and almost convincing response.

Howard's wife, Christine, is the most lovely and charming person you'd ever hope to meet. Sadly we saw her infrequently as Howard's life away from work was unfortunately not often shared with us. I choose to think that this was a factor of his character rather than a deliberate choice to exclude the un-washed from his extracurricular life, but I'm not completely sure about this. I did a stint at Dick Johnson Racing after my time at Nissan. Dick was one of the boys – after-work beers and occasional parties at his house were part of the scene. A very different experience to working for Howard. At time of writing, Dick is still with us and Howard is not. I wish for all our sakes that he'd been better at sharing his stresses and frustrations – bottling this stuff up often causes it to eat one up from inside, which is what led to him being taken from us.

There very often seemed to be some sort of deal going on in the background, often involving tyres or suspension struts or brakes or what have you. When we were at Braeside, someone would turn up at the workshop and tell us they'd come to pick up the tyres, or whatever, that Howard had organised. We'd know nothing about it so we'd have to ring head office to get the "oh yes, just give him four used 195/14s" or whatever it happened to be. Before that, at South Melbourne, probably because there were Nissan execs stationed there, these 'deals' would involve one of us dropping off components to a certain associated business in Brighton after hours.

I only discovered a few years ago that as part of the arrangement whereby the rally team was removed from Wilkinson at Hartwell and installed at South Melbourne under Marsden, all used components and tyres from the team would be disposed of through Wilkinson's DatsunSport business which had the franchise to sell Nissan competition parts in Australia. Bruce felt aggrieved when after a year or so he'd received zilch from the team and he apparently complained to Nissan management. When confronted, Howard stated bluntly that no, that wasn't going to happen. Apparently no one called him to account and Howard continued to use parts and tyres as currency for his own purposes – partly I'm sure though to grease the wheels with people he needed on-side.

Sometime around 1977 Howard approached me with a business proposal involving himself, John Armitage and myself. The plan involved John selling used rally bits from a shopfront, I would operate a workshop behind it, fitting the parts and doing other mods and Howard would, I guess, grease the wheels so to speak. We got as far as locating a premises in Canterbury before it all fell through – thank God! I don't remember why or why it was never spoken about again and sadly I have no way to find out as I'm the last man standing. It was just another slice of fortuitous luck on my journey with Nissan and I'm so happy everything worked out as it did.

When Howard left Nissan early in 1985, Paul Beranger, who took over his non-motorsport related role, found he needed to recover eleven Nissan vehicles that Howard had 'lent' to people all over the country. I don't know if the 11 included 4 rally Stanzas that ended up in the hands of rally hotshots from each of W.A., N.S.W., S.A. and QLD with no money changing hands. I gather Paul had fairly limited success.

I have no axe to grind. Howard treated me very well, forgave my shortcomings and allowed me the opportunity to learn an enormous amount. He was obviously well respected by the motorsport community and the motoring industry in general so much so that his memorial event over-filled a huge Melbourne city venue. I just don't want to let slip, the opportunity to 'balance the books' a little. He was not the omniscient God he was portrayed as by the motoring journalists of the day, nor the commentators on Facebook in more recent times. He was a guy who had a very clever knack of being able to give credit where it was due while giving the impression he was really just being magnanimous. I believe Howard enjoyed the game he sometimes played of offering maybe four parts truth, three parts invention to cover what he didn't know, and the rest just playful rubbish in order just to play with you.

Recently there was a retrospective article published in a glossy monthly and written by a journalist who's been around since our rallying days and who gave our team great mirth by how much of this 'Howie speak' he would absorb and what he wrote subsequently. A myth has developed over the years about the Nissan Bluebird Turbo's alleged facility to enable boost adjustment by the driver (contrary to the rules of the day). Some 16 years after HM's passing this journalist seemed convinced of the truth of a 'confession' from Howard that this was achieved by pulling the ashtray out to increase boost and pushing it back to reduce it. One of the funniest things I ever read. Thanks Howard, you keep on giving.

Richard Power's impression: *"An English gentleman of impeccably diplomatic manner who somehow found himself cornered in the world of motorsport. He used to respond to entreaties as to how to get into motorsport by asking how he could get out of it. Howard was a strategic thinker with an unerring eye to leveraging the sport for marketing effect."*

R.I.P. Howard, I wish I'd made the effort to thank you for your faith in me before you departed.

ROSS DUNKERTON

The most likeable bloke I ever met, he managed to make me feel like his best mate even as my brain told me that wasn't possible. I was invited to his wedding to Lisa in Perth and when I arrived they invited me to go on their honeymoon with them and wouldn't take no for an answer! Ross' navigator at the time, Steve McKimmie, one of the funniest guys you'll ever meet, also came. We towed his boat (Stanza II) up the WA coast to Shark Bay, stayed in a caravan he'd left at Monkey Mia, fished, explored, laughed and ate fresh seafood every day. It was amazing and I've not had a better holiday since.

He took me to rallies in New Caledonia, New Guinea, India and Malaysia. We did a Total Oil Sydney to Melbourne Economy Run together and he invited me to crew on his 1979 Repco Round Australia Trial Volvo campaign. (Most regrettably I was not able to go and have mourned missing that adventure ever since.) Ross, Peter Mackay and Geoff Jones finished fourth to the overwhelmingly better financed Holden Dealer Team's trifecta, after breakages and mechanical troubles that would have broken lesser men. It's not too much of an exaggeration to say that he dominated the poor Volvo's will and dragged it half the way, sometimes on three wheels.

While maybe not the tidiest of drivers, Ross' record shows that was no impediment and he more than made up for any deficiency in his style with determination and perseverance in spades plus truly prodigious road reading. Despite team ribbing that we wouldn't want to reincarnate as a Dunko throttle cable, often by creating his own good fortune, he bettered George's record of results with our team, notwithstanding Howard's attempts at dislodging him and often being given the seconds of available equipment.

Ross' wicked sense of fun was constantly at odds with our prim team manager who was frequently embarrassed about the goings on in the team. From drinking beer and shenanigans at the Sandcastle Hotel in Port Macquarie (Ross and Jeff hanging off the bar's balcony and holding up coasters with numbers to 'score' the girls passing below, all after a hard night's rallying and while supposed to be sleeping) to his irreverent post rally presentation talks, you could tell that Howard wasn't happy. If only Dunko would behave and maybe even allow the number one driver through sometimes, all would have been well, but nah, wasn't going to happen. Howard's problem was there was only one thing worse than having Dunko on your team – and that was having Dunko driving for the opposition!

Ross was so determined to be a winner that he trained for it – attending Toast Masters meetings in his hometown and practicing until he'd mastered his initially clumsy performances at post event presentations and become the undoubted highlight of these occasions. Ross would unfailingly have us all in stitches with his irreverent stories from the event, such that, I swear, even the opposition's service crews would be willing him on, hoping they'd be enjoying belly laughs and a beer with Dunko afterwards. Heaven forbid that George or Greg Carr would do well in an event and take up valuable speech time with their comparatively dull, on-stage speeches.

It seems to me that Ross was around for the whole time I was involved but when I look at the record now I see that he was only a member of the team for a few short years – the '75 Southern Cross and the '76 Australian Championship in the LHD 240Z. In 710s: one round of the ARC in '77 then a works car but with Gerry Ball Tuning support for the Cross that year, and then full support for the 1978 ARC series. In Stanzas he had works drives for the '78, '79 and '80 Southern Crosses and in between, Australian Championship events between December '78 and the end of '81. He also did a few special events for us during this time, notably the 1978 Castrol International in a hot-rodded Datsun 620 ute, the 1980 PNG Safari out of Port Moresby and the 1981 Macleay 1000 off-road race in two of the Stanzas.

If he wasn't competing in one of our cars you can be pretty sure between 1972 and 1977 he was competing at the top level in his own 240 or 260Z. Between 1974 and 1983 he won five Australian Rally Drivers Championships (including an equal first with George). He was also equal second in 1978 with Colin Bond and was third three times. That's nine out of 10 years on the podium! He also won the final Southern Cross Rally in 1980.

For 38 events in a works Datsun, Ross produced 10 wins, 9 seconds and 6 thirds – 25 podium finishes! If we add in the events he did in his own Datsun between 1974 and 1982, from a total of 56 events: 13 wins, 12 seconds, and 10 thirds – 35 podiums at the top level of rallying in Datsuns in Australia. Amazing!

Richard Power's summary: *The comedic larrikin of the Aus rally world for decades, 'Dunko's rally successes plus his antics and droll TV and live commentary attracted sponsors in his home state of WA where he was a rural Datsun dealer and hands-on rally car builder. His huge driving talent netted him many titles in Australia and wins in SE Asian events.*

JOHN LARGE

Between 1971 and 1976, when Jeff Beaumont took over, Ross was navigated by Perth phamascist, John Large. John was highly intelligent, driven and ambitious and the two of them became a near unbeatable team. They obtained sponsorship from Channel 9 in Perth and Ansett Airlines and won the 1975 Australian Championship as privateers over supported Datsun drivers, Stewart McLeod and George Fury. He was never shy of lodging an official protest to an event's Director if he felt they'd been disadvantaged in some way. I remember him as somewhat aloof but maybe that was due to his lasered focus on his role.

For 1976 Large became insistent that Datsun take them on as a paid crew. Probably in part at least due to timing, as Datsun was in process of transitioning to a corporatised rally team, they were denied, and quoting 'Dunko', " *...this was an afront to Large's considerable ego and he decided not to continue. Instead he entered into motor sport administration, eventually becoming President to the Confederation of Australian Motorsport (CAMS) and a Vice President of the Federation International l'Automibile (FIA).*"

Ross says of John, *"He was the most amazing navigator I ever knew."* High praise indeed!

JEFF BEAUMONT

With a terrific record of success between 1973 and 1981 at the top level in Datsuns, Jeff was one of our key team members. First with Bob Watson in a LHD 240Z in the 1973 Southern Cross and then with Rauno Aaltonen in three subsequent SCRs '76 and '77 in 710s and '78 in a Stanza.

Jeff became the slightly more serious faced, other-half of the Dunkerton/Beaumont team which had prodigious success for us in 240Zs, 710s and Stanzas between 1976 and '81. Together, Ross and Jeff won three Australian Rally Championships, '76, '77 and '79 (equal with Fury/Suffern in '77), were fourth in the '78 SCR, second in '79 and won the final 'Cross' in 1980. They scored 24 podium finishes between 1976 and 1981! The name Jeff Beaumont appears many times in these pages.

When we first met, Jeff was a sales rep for Ceilcote, a company in Devonport, Tasmania that made chemical resistant fibreglass products for industry. He later went on to create TechSport in Bayswater, Victoria, a business specialising in parts and motorsport preparation for the Mitsubishi Lancer Evos and has been a successful rally driver in his own right.

BILL EVANS

Very shortly after Howard joined Nissan and had visited the workshop, he either determined I needed a mentor or that the team needed more than a single mechanic to run two cars in the Australian Rally Championship, so he turned up at the workshop one day and introduced Bill Evans. Just when I thought my life couldn't be happier, here was another hero that I'd be working with.

Richard Power knew 'Wild Bill' at the time due to Richard's involvement with the Datsun Racing Team, and I do love his turns of phrase:

More racer than rallyist, wry and laconic Bill was fast regardless and sometimes campaigned a Datsun 120Y with some NMA help in rallies when he wasn't terrorizing the tiddler classes at Bathurst, Sandown and other series production car races of the era in the Datsun Racing Team's 1200s.

At this time Bill had been running his family business, the long established 'Evans Motors', in the southern Melbourne suburb of Brighton as well as driving for the Datsun Racing Team some weekends. I did wonder what string HM had at his disposal to draw Bill away from his business. I think there might have been more between those two than was shared with me…

When the Australian built 120Y was released in 1976, Nissan organised a press day at Calder Park Raceway so the journalists could test drive them on a closed road. Bill and I were asked to attend, I assume to handle any issues arising with the cars and probably to unload and reload the truck that took them out there. After the journos had done their thing and been escorted off by HM, Bill suggested we do some laps in one of the pre-thrashed cars.

He took me around for some quick ones (for a standard 120Y) and then insisted I have a go. So, with Bill navigating the lines and enforcing the braking points I got to do about four fast laps and can clearly remember my right knee shaking profoundly as we charged toward turn one with Bill insisting I stay 'pedal to the metal' way past where I wanted to be on the brakes. The things you remember! Anyway he said I'd done pretty well so that put a smile on my dial.

Bill returned to Evans Motors before the Southern Cross that year so that, with the whirlwind my life had become, it seemed like no time at all before he was gone again, although he did make a comeback to co-drive the Nissan Patrol hotrod in the 1977 BP Desert Rally with Peter Wherrett. It's been terrific to catch up with him again in recent years.

Bill Evans dominating the up to 1300cc class at the Hardie Ferodo 1000 at Bathurst in 1974

BARRY NELSON

Baz joined us mid way through 1976 as a replacement for Bill Evans. He'd been working for Alan Moffat, building and maintaining his Mustang in the U.S. and came under the notice of Howard while they were both over there playing with V8s.

Baz was the stereo-typical Australian motorsport engineer of the day – light-weight and fabrication finesse were not yet so highly prized as they later became. No problems, we had just the project to suit. Having seen the hotrod service vans operating in European rallying, Howard reckoned that something should be done with our underpowered E20 service vans.

Barry had the gas axe out in a flash cutting away the box section behind and above the original 4-cylinder push-rod engine on E20 #1 and lengthening the gear change rods with a couple of bits of angle iron. We sourced a used L24 (240K) motor from Datspares, raised it up into position from underneath (crane through the doorway) welded up some engine mounts to suit its upright stance and bolted it in. He threw away the standard carburettor and bolted on an adaptor for a twin-barrel Holley carb and mashed up a rather rudimentary air filter that turned into the least reliable part of the project. He removed the sump and cut & shut one side to straighten up the bottom of the pan.

Once happy with the power plant, it was onto the brakes. Front hubs from the rally cars fitted straight onto E20 stub axles and the Sumitomo 4-spot callipers were somehow adapted to the uprights. 14" rally wheels with old rally tyres were bolted to the 4-stud hubs. For the rear, only the axles and brake drums needed to be drilled to suit the 4-stud wheels and boom – it was done. It seemed to take no time at all. The engine proved a bit too heavy for the standard torsion bars though and Baz had to organise to have some heavier ones made. By luck or good judgement they were almost spot on and these endured till some time after the team disbanded.

Proving a success Baz was then asked to do another conversion on an E20 belonging to a bloke from Girling Brakes in Sydney. Heaven knows what that deal was all about.

Baz says, "It was a turquoise blue with white roof – Howard arranged it. I think it was one of his contra deals. Peter Thorn, who was in America with Allan Moffat and myself, also did some paint work for him. I did the motor conversion and brakes. Howard also gave Peter Thorn some afterhours work in conjunction with Paul Beranger. Peter and I still hang out together."

In 1977, Baz did the lion's share of the work in the conversion of a new (but very old-looking) G60 Nissan Patrol that was to be run in the BP Desert Rally at Hattah in North Western Victoria. In short order he'd ripped out the huge 6-cyl, 4 litre engine, the enormous gearbox and transfer case, and the way-heavy front diff and axles. It became a shadow of its former self. After plating the hole where the front diff came from, he slipped in an LR18 rally engine (saved from one of the 710s that had to be scrapped) and 5-speed, 'Option 1' gearbox. A 'Baz-built' roo bar was bolted to the front, Bilstein shockers underneath and 4-point seat belts inside – almost instant off-road rally car. Peter Wherrett and Bill Evans were the crew and the Patrol was painted up with 'Torque DESERT PATROL' and flash stripes in order to look the part for the episode of Wherrett's 'Torque' TV program that was made.

Later that year, George Fury had the idea of building a DeDion, 4-link rear axle for the 710 – another good project for the Baz. While we were away on the Cross that year, Baz had a 710 shell on a rotisserie and whipped up the required components so that, by the time the rest of the team returned from the Cross, they were ready to bolt in and test. George liked the feel but he was no quicker over our test distance at Mt Slide and, as the Stanza wasn't far away, it was decided to abandon the project.

Baz can tell you about why it was he had to leave us early in 1978:

"I did not leave on good terms because of something I said at the 200B release at Calder Park. I was quoted in Auto Action as saying the difference between the 180B and the new 200B was twenty more mistakes. Lionel Sparrow was pissed which led to my sacking." [Lionel Sparrow was one of the top execs at Nissan and we always seemed to be running afoul of him in one way or another – until he was caught pinching petrol from the company bowser, we believe in a failed attempt to set us up.]

The Auto Action quote was a typical wisecrack from the Baz but sadly this time it came back to bite him. He'd been a great character and morale booster in the team and we'd miss him.

GREG CARR & WAYNE GREGSON

It's been difficult to decide where, and even if, to place Greg in my chronological order as he'd had so much success in Datsuns from as early as 1973, but when he reached prominence on the national level it was with the yellow, privately-run 180B SSS that was built up in Canberra from the mechanicals of the Kilfoyle-crashed, 1975 Akademos Rally 180B SSS. His only full Datsun works drives were late 1976 when he was lent a 710 for the Holden Dealers International and the Alpine but even so, ran under the Gerry Ball Tuning banner and with their service support.

In 1977 Greg began his force majeure with the Ford team and so became our fierce adversary. He could not be denied though and has managed to elbow his way into my chronology with this brief biog.

Greg was an unassuming Canberra public servant statistician. In 1974, running a Datsun 1600 and mentored by tuning shop proprietor, Gerry Ball, Greg and navigator Wayne Gregson won the Bunbury Curran Rally (then a round of the Australian Championship) and then in 1975 also the Don Capasco Rally (later named the Castrol International Rally) for the first of six consecutive times!

In 1975 Carr placed third outright in the Southern Cross Rally in the yellow 180B SSS. Still with that car they went on to win the Kleber Alpine in '75 and The Castrol International Rally in early '76, then placed third in the Open class for The Marchall Rally, straight afterwards.

Later in '76, for The North Eastern Rally (also an ARC round) Gerry Ball Tuning was lent the 710 that Wherrett had used in the Castrol that year – Greg and Wayne placed third in the Open class. Then later, they crashed out early in the 'Cross' but were able to repair in time to win The Holden Dealers International with this 710.

For the Kleber Alpine Rally in '76 they were lent the 710 Fury/Suffern had been using for the '76 Australian Rally Championship and they produced another good win.

Greg and Wayne were rather bashful characters and Gerry Ball I found to be rather gruff and unfriendly. I don't think I ever had more than a few words with any of them. Ball had an eye for driving talent in his patch though, having also previously supported the Canberran Comet Peter Lang and then Mark Hankinson from Bega.

Bruce Wilkinson must have had a better relationship with Ball though and helped him out with parts and even lent cars on occasions. I think that, when Howard replaced Bruce, the relationship may have become less cordial and from our team's perspective the Gerry Ball Tuning team was more opponent than ally.

Carr's prodigious talent was rewarded when he was signed by Colin Bond to drive an Escort RS2000 for the new Ford works rally team. Greg had his first ARC round win with the Ford works team in the 1977 Bega Valley Rally and led the Southern Cross Rally that year until late on the last night when forced to retire with alternator failure.

In 1978 Greg won the ARC for the Ford team in a series-long battle with Dunkerton and Fury in what is widely regarded as a classic period of Australian rallying. Carr won numerous rallies during his four years at the Ford rally team, including four victories in the Castrol International.

In 1980 he again went close to winning the 'Cross', finishing second to Dunkerton and ahead of teammate world rally champion, Ari Vatanen. The Ford works rally team was wound up at the end of the 1980 season.

Though very fast, it could not be said he had a great deal of sympathy for his machinery. After one particular episode in the 1980 Southern Cross Rally, fellow competitor and great character, Ed Mulligan, re-christened him, Rex D Carr.

After having recently read the published accounts of all the events Greg and Wayne did together at the top level, I didn't see one mention of their losing time on a wrong road – the best testament for a navigator.

It was interesting to note that, for those heady years of rallying, both Ford and Datsun had their reserved and unassuming, as well as their outgoing and gregarious drivers – Greg a good match for George Fury in this regard, Colin Bond for Ross Dunkerton.

Richard Power can have the last word: *"Maybe it was Greg working off the frustrations of a career in the Canberra public service bureaucracy that drove him so hard and fast in a rally car! But fast he was, just ask the international stars. Much slower to dip into his pocket though, according to proximate sources."*

JAMIE DRUMMOND

Born 1955 Jamie was a country boy from Walwa in Victoria, just up-river a bit and on the other side of the Murray from George Fury's farm at Talmalmo. Truly magnificent country.

He'd done his motor mechanic apprenticeship in Albury and had come to the notice of Fury some time in 1975. Captivated by his general enthusiasm (I'd suggest) George would have recommended him to Howard as a suitable young addition to our team and he showed up in Melbourne as we were moving the rally team to the much larger premises at Braeside in Melbourne's south east at the end of 1975. We became great mates immediately. Here are some details extracted from emails between us (with only minor edits for clarity) in the last months before his passing:

"When I had my interview with Howard early in 1975, he offered me 4 different jobs – Bob Jane, Alan Moffat, Frank Gardner and Nissan. He gave me one month to decide!

I left my job in Albury in the middle of 1975 and moved to North Dandenong, in SE suburbs of Melbourne. I travelled into South Melbourne every day for a few months. Howard got me a job just servicing cars there. That's where I first met you. He told me it might take a little time before I could join the Rally Team because of the planned move out to Braeside etc. I was like a deer in the headlights and was hanging on his every word but I remember thinking: Is this really going to happen? I got the impression he was making it up as he spoke. So I asked him if I could get a job closer to Dandenong. He agreed and got me a job at an Ampol service station in Mentone!! He kept saying I couldn't start with the rally team full time. I think he was stringing me along for a while.

I'd work at Mentone then drive in to South Melbourne after hours and help you pack up for the move. You were the only one there, I've no idea where Barry [Nelson] was. And then after a few months Howard told me that my full time employment had been approved and I started with you at Braeside!"

I really don't think I would have been employed if it wasn't for

George F and also me being super keen helping and learning at night after work!

I wouldn't change a thing though! Except maybe losing my licence for 2 and a half years…" [I'll spare you, and his memory, the details]

Jamie was a great addition to our team, hardworking, enthusiastic and a straight shooter – he knew what a spade was for and he knew what to call it. And if the job needed spade work he was the first to grab a spade. This was in the days before we had adopted our specialties, when it was all hands on deck to be ready for the next event, whatever that took.

The first of our 6-cyl E20 service vans became his. He drove it with enthusiasm, as with everything, and looking back, you'd have to say that, in the end, he'd been pretty lucky to make it to 64 years. More than one teammate applied to Howard for a transfer after being assigned to team up with him in 'his' E20.

This book was to have been a joint project between the two of us, he had a good memory and we thought we could create a terrific book combining our talents. As it turned out I got very little from Jamie before we lost him. R.I.P. mate – if only I'd attacked the project with the same vigour you were known for…

"I've got a good memory! [well, better than mine anyway] *And there's a lot more great times I can reflect on! I think you and I should write a book about our time at Nissan Motor Sport! I'll drag up the memories and you can write and configure the book! It would be a best seller! We have plenty of characters to choose from!"*

PETER DAVIS

Pete Davis left his suspension business and joined us, initially part-time, in 1977. Howard's motivation in bringing him on board was, I'm sure, largely to provide expertise in our efforts to soften the 710's suspension. It was he who began re-valving struts and shocks and then re-gassing them. Pete was also involved in our 710 light-weighting endeavours and then, when Barry Nelson had to go, Pete took over his position in 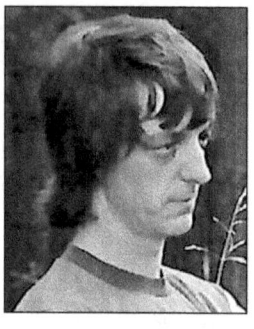 the workshop and in the van with Jamie, which did not go well and led to his resigning before the 'Cross' in '79.

It was with the Stanza though that he was to play a pivotal role. I'll let him tell this snippet of his story which he has kindly provided.

"... we received the Stanza early 78 which if you remember George put off Mt. Slide with Howard in the car during initial testing. I have a photo of you/us winching our guts out on a Tirfor getting it back up onto the road.

I think it's first Australian Championship outing was Bega where the diff failed and we realised the aluminium housings were not up to the job and [from then on] used steel housings instead.

You guys then fitted the twin cam to the Stanza and the rest is history. I particularly remember the car being almost cut in half just prior to loading it for Sydney when the tailshaft broke on Governor Road [a straight stretch of back road near the Braeside workshop we used for high-speed testing, or a quick trip up to Nissan Head Office in South Dandenong]. I was at the dentist and when I got back to Braeside expecting the car to be gone, instead it was in a million bits with bodies working all over it. In the end Jamie and I had to trailer it to Sydney. As you know we went on to win the event."

I remember thinking it was tragic that we lost Pete Davis mostly because he was not able to cope with Jamie's 'enthusiastic' driving. Pete had made a terrific contribution to our team and played a key role both in the Australian development of the Stanza as well as George and Monty's fantastic Cross win in '78. He went back to his successful motorsport suspension business.

Pete's lovely wife Val worked at Nissan's Head Office for these and later years and interestingly was able to salvage much of their collection of racing and rallying trophies and photographs from a rubbish skip after a big clean out. How dare they!! But how lucky to have had someone on hand to save it all.

PETER RYAN

Pete Ryan joined the team before the 1978 Southern Cross, coming to us via Bill Evans' Evans Motors, where he worked for a period after finishing his motor mechanic apprenticeship, interestingly initially with Melbourne Airport's Fire Department. Pete was introduced to Howard by Richard Power (then of Nissan's Marketing department). I'd be surprised if he didn't also introduce him to Bill Evans considering the connection to the Datsun Racing Team.

Pete and I teamed up in the second of the two 6-cylinder E20 vans, he settling into the driving seat and I shuffling the maps. Pete is around 6'1" tall and, other than Howard who could look at him eye to eye, the rest of us were at a bit of a disadvantage in that regard. We had many fun, exciting, scary times together and saw many bleary eyed dawns.

In the workshop, following Pete Davis' departure, Pete took responsibility for the gearboxes and diffs and he slotted right in. He seemed to have a knack though, of saying something derogatory or taking the mickey just as Howard walked in through the door – he got caught time after time.

Pete left at the end of 1981 just as we were finishing the transition to a race team, he moved to Sydney for a few years to join Colin Bond's team, racing Alfa Romeo GTVs.

We've remained firm friends ever since.

PETER ANDERSON

Pete Anderson, Dave Thompson and myself had, in our early 20s, belonged to the Sportscar Owners Club of Victoria (SOCV). Pete and I were the quiet types, Thommo rather more rowdy. I'd lost contact with Pete but not Dave thankfully, so that when we really needed a full time welder/fabricator at the beginning of 1981, Dave was able to point us toward one of the best there is.

Pete had been a champion sailor and had turned his hand to repairing boat fittings and making parts. No welding or fabrication job was beyond him it seemed, and he took the quality of our new 1980 Stanza to a whole other level which carried forward into the Bluebirds. We were proud to roll them off the trailer or out of our transporter and display the workmanship.

When Jamie lost his driver's licence for two and a half years, Pete picked him up and drove him home from work every day. Jamie credited him with saving his career.

After the motorsport days had passed Pete left Melbourne to return to his roots – starting a boating oriented fabricating business in Queensland's Airlie Beach on the Whitsunday Coast. In the intervening years, Pete has produced several of the stainless steel artwork pieces on public display in and around Airlie Beach – testaments to his prodigious skill, one and all.

Real soon now he'll get onto finishing his beautiful trimaran sailboat and finally do some cruising around the Whitsundays.

He and vivacious and steadfast partner, Rhonda have created a tropical paradise on seven acres of rain forest just west of Airlie and enjoy it still.

GEORGE SMITH

A Tasmanian who'd struck out for the mainland with his child bride, George Smith was a part of Colin Bond's Ford Rally Team when we met him in 1977. He'd been fairly seriously burned in a pit lane fire with Alan Moffat's Falcon at Bathurst in 1978 but made a full recovery. I seem to remember that, at the end of 1979 he was disgruntled at Bondy's and was keen for a new challenge.

So, being one man short after Pete Davis' departure we approached George and he jumped at the opportunity. He relocated the family, wife Jan, seven year-old daughter, Angie, two year-old Peter, and Julianne, nine months, from Sydney to Dingley, not far from our workshop at Braeside.

With his racing experience he'd seen the better build quality of the race-cars of the time and, with a budget to work with, set about raising the standard of our Stanza's fabrication and presentation. The new Stanza we built from a body shell early in 1980 quickly reflected his and Peter Anderson's workmanship. I think it would be no exaggeration to say George taught us how to spend Nissan's money, something he had a flair for and took pretty seriously once we began racing.

A bit of a larrikin, George loved a drink after work and though I jest a little, he took relish in captaining the team in that regard, finding every chance to knock back a few on the company's dime. I reckon I'd have been able to remember quite a bit more of our years together had I not become tangled in all that. "You boys are becoming very expensive", we heard more than once from the guy who ended up with the bills on his desk.

Rather than being put off by Jamie's driving, George encouraged his daredevil antics. How the two of them came out of all that unscathed, mystifies me.

In the racing years, while I was ensconced in my spacious engine room at Healey Road, George had taken responsibility for the gearboxes and general fabrication as well as an unofficial workshop foreman role. I'd have to say that he could rightly claim more than his fair share of the successes we enjoyed with the turbo Bluebirds.

GEOFF PORTMAN & ROSS RUNNALLS

Victorian foresters from Alpine Rally country in north east Victoria, Geoff and Ross, supported by Les Collins' growing engineering skills, quickly rose to prominence with increasing levels of support from Howard Marsden.

Ross and Geoff, here at one of their many happy hunting grounds – this one the Bright Sports Club.

So, after spending a couple of years under our wing, Geoff and Ross were finally made card-carrying members of the Datsun Rally Team midway through 1980 in time for the Bega Valley Rally, in which they placed fourth. The Donlee Rally was the next and last round for the year and they won it convincingly.

It was no secret that Geoff was held in high regard by Howard and by late 1979 he'd been dodging increasingly blunt questions from motoring journalists about when 'Portholes' would get a drive for the factory team.

I guess trying to do his bit to secure an ARC title win for George, HM saw the opportunity to protect Fury's points tally by adding Geoff to the team and giving the Ford team someone else they needed to beat. Geoff and Ross did the job nicely, winning the final round and allowing George's third place to clinch the title.

For the Southern Cross in 1980 they were given the Stanza George and Monty had used in the Motogard Rally in NZ and looked, at the halfway point, as though they'd have a convincing win. Early in Divison 3 though, things began to unravel when Geoff ran wide at a crest and a log reached out and bit him, breaking the steering and costing them dearly before repairs could be affected. At end Div 3 they'd dropped to sixth place but worse was in store in Div 4 when the engine stopped due to another valve drivetrain failure.

1981 would be another story though as they swept all before them winning Victorian Trials Championship, Victorian Rally Championship and Australian Rally Championship.

I was fortunate to have had an opportunity to navigate for Geoff in two events in 1982. I was left with the impression that I'd been the calmest I'd ever felt in a rally car, such was his smoothness and surety.

Geoff and Ross had careers full of many highlights. They were an incredible team. Ross is still arguably the best in Australia with maps but also more than fluent in route charts and pace notes. Geoff was arguably the very best Australian rally driver. In works Datsun Stanzas and in some of the many privately run vehicles he drove, usually built and prepared by brother-in-law, Les Collins and his Datrally team, they were, all being well, near unbeatable. R.I.P. Geoff, we'll miss you.

✣ ✣ ✣ ✣ ✣

There were several part-time team members who came to events or just stepped in to help us out.

Here I must begin with Randall Cooke who was Bruce Wilkinson's business partner and Hartwell Datsun's Service Manager. Bruce describes him as a wizard with cars. His name keeps popping up with reverence in early Datsun Rally Team stories, but sadly, I don't remember ever meeting him and he is no longer with us.

Another of Bruce's helpers on the Southern Cross rallies back then was Graham Hensell who assisted with service planning.

Someone who stood out in our crowd of supporters was lanky, Richard Power. Richard came with the package from Wilkinson Motors although he actually worked for NMA and, as he says, *"As the only person under MD George Denner, so motivated (except for rallyist Bruce Wilson, NMA's Datsun Sales Centre manager downstairs), I got a gig to handle the journos on events.*

Power, by now in perfectly cut red overalls, pandering to Peter Wherrett in the '76 Castrol Int'l.

Datsun dealer and racer John Roxburgh prepared the press cars so I got to know him, his other drivers, Doug Whiteford, Bill Evans and journo James Laing-Peach, plus his imported race mechanics Carlheinz Schwab from Germany and Hans Blaser from Switzerland. I volunteered to help in the pits at Sandown, Adelaide and Bathurst. Rockerbox issued me with undersized overalls, eliciting a negative comment from George Denner pit side." [But I've allowed him to digress...]

"As the '72 'Cross approached, I visited Bruce Wilkinson's Datsun dealership in Hartwell to check out the works rally cars and did my bit applying all the event and sponsor decals including on the service 260C wagons. I was sent on every 'Cross up to and including the '77. By then, I'd been unwillingly moved into fleet sales so I left NMA after getting a PR gig at Ford in '78." I very much appreciate Richard's eloquent additions to this book and his memories and insight into the early times.

Back in the early days, John Bosua always seemed to be where DRT cars were. He was there at Wilkinson Motors and he was the first bloke we called when we needed another pair of skilled hands at an event up until 1977.

John Bosua with Shekhar Mehta's '73 South'n Cross 240Z

When it was decided to convert a 620 ute into a rally car, John was the man for the job. He had an auto repair business in Vermont, Victoria, named BGM Motors – perfect for the odd overflow job.

The second man we called in those days was John Armitage – I've enjoyed seeing him pop up in photos of the '75 Don Capasco and the '76 Castrol at least.

In the early days, Stan Holmes used to be the man for gearbox and diff overhauls and then, from 1976 onward until the end of our race team days, Victorian Rally Champs, Chris and Simon Brown, were regular helpers willing to take on any job. They became great mates of our team.

JRA in action at the '76 Castrol

Younger brother of Richard, Chris Power and I drove our 1600s to the '73 Southern Cross as spectators and became fully hooked. In 1977 he got to drive Källström's 1974 Cross 710 around the service route of the SCR to advance reserve (read rope-off) the best service areas for our following crews.

For 1976 and '77 we had large teams with several helpers. Those I've been able to I.D. in photos were Bill Evans' mate, Sunshine Sam,

Identifiable here at Port Macquarie in 1977, from left: Chris Brown, Simon Brown, Pete Ryan, Nick Watt (tall) and myself (less so).

Bob Suffern (Monty's brother), Mark Holmes (my driver for events when I got time off to compete), Pete Ryan (before he joined us full-time late in '78), Bob Bird (Victorian rally driver), and Nick Watt (mechanic from the Datsun Service Centre), who also co-serviced with me on Dunko's 260Z in the '76 New Caledonian Safari. He also crewed with Gerry Ball's team in a couple of ARC rounds that year. Steve Hollowood's younger brother, Duncan used to come to the Braeside workshop and help us pack up for events.

Ray Francis was a friend of Bruce Wilkinson's and had a furniture removal business in Melbourne. Between 1974 and at least '77 he transported our wheels and tyres (up to 200 of them) plus our luggage from Melbourne to Port Macquarie and back. Then,

after a hard night of rallying and too little sleep he'd be gently knocking at our Sandcastle Motel room door until we were awake and he knew we were up and going. In later years he brought along daughter, Gaye, who provided refreshments along the route and helped to keep us going. She found and married John Gray – one of the Ford team guys.

In early 1978, after we lost Barry Nelson, Pete Pender stepped in to fill his role on events until Peter Ryan joined us full-time before the Cross. And then in '79 Dave Thompson joined us part-time when we wanted to make wet sumps and other fabricated bits for the Stanzas. Auto-electrician Graeme (Jackie) Stewart, who'd been keeping our alternators and starters in good shape for some time, joined the team intermittently to take over the Bluebird Turbo wiring loom construction and modifications – something I'd been responsible for until then.

There will be others I've not remembered and I apologise. Please let me know if you're able to help complete the record – I can add names for the next printing. Honest – the whole next page is blank!

International Southern Cross DRIVERS

RAUNO AALTONEN

Known world-wide as the 'Flying Finn', Rauno often arrived earlier and stayed on later than the other international drivers we had in the team. He was always keen to go out testing and participate in shakedown events. He is such a friendly and gentle man and his English so impeccable it was always like rekindling a still-warm friendship when he arrived each year. I met up with him at an event some years after the team had disbanded and he impressed the hell out of me by remembering my name and warmly shaking my hand.

Between 1972 and 1979 Rauno ran works Datsuns in six 'Crosses', coming second in a 240Z in '72, finally winning the Cross for Nissan in a 710 in '77 and placing third in our team's '79 Stanza trifecta. In 1972 Rauno was teamed with Steve Halloran, an Australian who'd had success in SCRs and had become something of a specialist navigator for internationals. Then, in 1975, Rauno brought John Souminen to co-drive with him. For '76, '77 and '78 he was partnered by Jeff Beaumont, further strengthening team relationships, until Jeff and Dunko became inseparable and Rauno did the 1979 Cross with Adrian Mortimer.

Richard Power says: *One of the original 'Flying Finns', Rauno had a professorial air and spoke very quietly, belying his ferocity behind the wheel. Among his many victories were the '65 Monte Carlo and the '66 Bathurst 500 in Mini Coopers, and the '77 'Cross in a 710. When young hopefuls asked him for the secret to his speed, he would simply say "Change Up!" He taught some of us groupies how to do a high speed reverse-to-second gear flick, handy for fleeing rampaging bull elephants comin' straight at ya!*

HARRY KÄLLSTRÖM

Harry was no Rauno and had only rudimentary English but he usually wore a cheeky smile that was somewhat endearing. I never really had the opportunity to socialise with him but now wish I'd made more of an effort in that regard. He was usually very fast – always immediately on the pace from the flag fall – but not the most sympathetic to his equipment, his record at SCRs was four DNFs (three engine failures) and one second place (in the '77 trifecta).

Harry was partnered in 1974, '75 and '76 by Roger Bonhomme and then in 1977 and '78 by Swede, Claes Bilstam

Richard Power described him thus: *Somewhat hunched Harry looked like a weathered, hard drinking old Viking, twirling his moustache with a mischievous glint in his eye. The '69 European Rally Champion in a Lancia Fulvia HF, his sole WRC win was the '76 Acropolis in a 710. He died aged 70 in 2009. His wife Sonja was a tall, Nordic Viqueen from Lappland in far north Sweden with a sense of humour and a guitar. She used to tell us: "You know in Sveeden, in der sommer time, vee go fishink and make lov; in der vinter time, vee can't go fishink...."*

SHEKHAR MEHTA

Shekhar came to us as a Datsun superstar having already won an East African Safari Rally and his huge, larger-than-life smile and apparent gladness to re-acquaint each time he came made him especially welcome.

I remember him telling a group of us about how tummy upsets were common for crews in the East African Safaris and diarrhoea often the result. Stopping though was only an option for losers so they let it go and opened the windows a bit. Whoa, too much info!

Shekhar's Southern Cross record was a DNF due to rear end damage in the RHD 240Z in 1973, third in a 710 in 1976, and sixth in the LZ16 engined PB210 in the seven-car effort for 1977. He was partnered by Roger Bonhomme in 1973 and Adrian Mortimer in '76 and '77.

Richard Power says of him: *A Ugandan-then-Kenyan of Indian descent and son of a wealthy family, Shekhar was a funny, sunny and canny personality who was especially good at long distance events, piloting 240Z's second Safari win in '73 then later winning another four in '79-'82 in Datsun 160Js/Nissan Violet GTs. He died of various illnesses in 2006 aged just 60.*

There were a few characters from the Datsun Rally Team who didn't really play leading roles in my time with the team but were heroes non-the-less and should be recognised here.

Edgar Herrmann ran a semi-works Datsun 1600 with Hans Schuller in the Ampol Trial of 1970. He returned in 1972 to drive a full works 180B SSS, this time navigated by Mike Mitchell and he stayed on for the Dulux Rally after the Cross and was navigated this time by Roger Bonhomme.

Tony Fall paid us a fleeting visit with a big reputation in 1973 to drive one of the works 240Zs and was navigated by Steve Halloran. They tipped the Z over early on the first night and weren't seen much subsequently. I overheard him chuckling about it with Shekhar Mehta which I thought was rather unfortunate.

Frank Kilfoyle, nearing the end of a stellar career mostly in Ford Cortinas, drove a works 610 in the 1973 Cross and also the Alpine, both with Mike Osborne navigating. In 1974 he drove a 710 in the Cross with Ian Richards but rolled early in Div 1 and DNF'd. Still pretty quick but was beginning to struggle to finish an event.

Bob Watson's first Datsun works drive also came in the 1973 Southern Cross Rally where he partnered with Jeff Beaumont in one of the LHD 240Zs. They placed a credible eighth in very trying conditions. In 1977 he drove a 710 supported by Gerry Ball's team, and with Peter Godden navigating, they placed third in the 710 trifecta that year.

In 1976 and '77, Nissan took a chance on a couple of super speed demons along with the usuals for the Southern Cross. Neither of them showed any interest in socialising with the larger team (Per-inge due no doubt to language difficulty) so I can't claim to have known them.

In 1976 the young hero, Per-inge Walfridsson arrived and started Car #16 with Peter Godden navigating. Per-inge proved to be reasonably quick but took a heavy toll on the car, rolling early and side-swiping a large tree later in the event. They persisted though and were rewarded with sixth place.

In 1977 Nissan went for the top shelf and a whole lot of experience and sent out Timo Makinen and Henry Liddon to get the job done – they were seeded, and ran, as Car #1. The event was notable for the fierce battle between Makinen and Greg Carr and at half distance Makinen was second to Greg by just 40 seconds. Div 3 provided minor troubles for Timo but Div 4 much more serious ones and he was forced out with a split sump.

...and the NAVIGATORS

Seldom the heroes but nevertheless indispensible.

Mike Mitchell – Herrmann 1972

Steve Halloran – Aaltonen 1972 & Fall 1973

Roger Bonhomme – Wilkinson 1972, Mehta 1973 & Källström 1974, 1975, 1976

Mike Osborne – Kilfoyle 1973

Ian Richards – Kilfoyle 1974

John Suominen – Aaltonen 1975

Jeff Beaumont – Aaltonen 1976, 1977, 1978 & Dunkerton 1979, 1980

Adrian Mortimer – Mehta 1976, Dunkerton 1978 & Aaltonen 1979

Claes Billstam – Källström 1977, 1978

Henry Liddon – Makinen 1977

Peter Godden – Per inge Walfridsson 1976 & Watson 1977

Geoff Pigram – Dunkerton 1977

The STORY
firstly a précis of my years employed by Nissan

1973-75: I worked as a Service Advisor at the Datsun Service Centre at the top of Elizabeth Street, Melbourne, and then in Sturt Street, South Melbourne, when it moved to larger premises. In my spare time I helped Bruce Wilson prepare and service his 1600 rally car.

Sept/Oct 1975: Helped out after hours at Wilkinson Motors with preparations for the Southern Cross Rally (from herein abreviated to the SCR or the Cross) and then went on the event as part of the Service Crew.

1976: Soon after the Service Centre moved to the larger facility in South Melbourne, I was approached by Vice President NMA, Sasamoto san, and told I should be the mechanic for the soon to be corporatised Datsun Rally Team, and which would be run out of our premises. Howard Marsden was soon after recruited as Team Manager.

Bill Evans joined the team not long after Howard arrived and then, when Bill couldn't continue to spare time away from his business, he was replaced by Barry Nelson (ex Alan Moffat and Howard). Barry did the first L24 conversion to one of our E20 vans. We had three 710s plus the LHD works 240Z that Sasamoto had arranged for Dunkerton.

We did the Castrol and four Australian Championship (ARC) rounds plus a couple of more minor events before three new 710s and the Japanese crew arrived for the SCR. George was leading in the Cross but DNF'd* late with a diff failure. Cowan won for Mitsubishi in a Lancer.

Considerably helped by the ARC regulations at that time which saw the LHD works 240Z eligible for championship points while the 710 was not, Dunko and Beauy easily won the ARC, doubling the points of second place.

At the end of 1976 we moved to a much larger workshop in Lower Dandenong Rd. Braeside and Jamie Drummond joined us full-time.

1977: By this time I'd taken responsibility for the engines. This was one of the great years for the ARC – hard-fought and very competitive between Datsun and Ford. Dunkerton/Beaumont led the series as a privateer until the third round in Queensland where his engine lost oil and seized.

Howard lent him a 710 for the rest of the series, which he ran under the Gerry Ball Tuning banner, Ross paying costs. Dunkerton/Beaumont and Fury/Suffern tied for the title that year.

Peter Davis joined us in the second half of the year and from this point we began Australian development of the works cars, particularly the cars' suspensions.

Despite our clean sweep of podium places in the SCR that year, Fury crashed out in spectacular fashion within sight of the end and Dunkerton was out in Division 3 with a failed differential while running tenth. Aaltonen won with Källström second and Watson third, all in 710s.

Mostly completed at Johnnie Bosua's BGM Motors in Vermont, we hot-rodded a Datsun 620 ute for Ross to drive in the '78 Castrol.

1978: The Castrol International in March was a bit of a hoot with Ross and Adrian Mortimer in the Datsun ute. It suffered rear shocker mount breakages as well as poor traction in the wet event and finished mid-field.

For the ARC we began the year with 710s and transitioned to Stanzas, first for Fury, midyear, and then Dunkerton later in the ARC season. Dunko finished the season on equal points with Greg Carr but Carr was awarded the title on count back. Fury placed fourth. It was another very compelling and hard-fought series.

Before the Southern Cross, mechanic Peter Ryan joined the team to replace Barry Nelson who'd blotted his copy book and was asked to resign.

1978 was our first SCR with Stanzas and this time Fury ran a comprehensively Australian-developed car including an L20B based DOHC engine and disc brake rear end. George and Monty had a famous victory. Dunkerton/Mortimer came fourth and won the Group 2 class with a Japanese SOHC motor. Aaltonen's and Källström's DOHC engines both expired with broken connecting rods.

1979: Was another fantastic ARC series with Dunkerton/Beaumont, at last full members of our team, clearly winning, with Fury/Suffern equal fourth with Geoff Portman/Ross Runnalls.

We also had a fantastic Southern Cross – George and Monty's second win, again with one of my engines. Topping it off, Dunkerton/Beaumont placed second and Aaltonen/Mortimer third, this time all with DOHC motors. A brilliant year, the only downer, Fury's DNF at the Castrol with a failed engine after flattening his exhaust on a rock.

Hugely talented fabricator/welder, Pete Anderson joined us late in the year, leading to big improvements in our cars' build quality.

1980: At the beginning of the year we successfully poached George Smith from the 'winding down' Ford team. He teamed up with Jamie in their pursuit E20 and was to be influential in both the Datsun Rally Team and Nissan Sport's racing efforts. My first project for the year was car preparation for the Total Oil Economy Run. A Sunny, a Stanza and a Bluebird, and I was rewarded with participating in the event with Ross Dunkerton in the Stanza, achieving 36.5 MPG.

We once again dominated the ARC. This time George and Monty had a clear points win from Colin Bond/John Dawson-Damer in their RS1800 BDG-powered Escort. Dunkerton/Beaumont were placed third and Portman/Runnalls, fourth.

The 1980 Southern Cross Rally was destined to be the last and it was won by Dunkerton/Beaumont, beating out our archrivals, the Ford team, Greg Carr and Ari Vatenen second and third.

We shipped a Stanza to Port Moresby for Ross and I to run in the 1980 PNG Independence Safari Rally in December.

1981: Early in the year we received a near new, independent rear suspension (IRS) Bluebird Turbo and began stripping it to build a Group C Touring Car racer. Work progressed as time permitted with the rally calendar.

With little in the way of works rally competition, it was decided to run the lead contender Stanza with an L20B SOHC engine (under Group A regs which actually became PRC) and painted up to match the Stanza SSS then available in Datsun showrooms. Dunko was again downgraded to factory-supported (basically the loan of a car) and Portman promoted to works driver. Portman dominated – four wins from his four ARC starts.

Pete Anderson and I flew to WA to support Dunkerton who won this first ARC event of the year in his borrowed Stanza. Portman/Runnalls won the series on 80 points, Fury/Suffern were second on 42 and Dunkerton/Beaumont were third on 35. Fury's Stanza was doing double duty as it was also being used in the occasional sports sedan race as George was being 'repurposed' as a racing driver. The car missed two ARC rounds due to damage from one race at Amaroo Park early June.

Dunko was given a Stanza to run at the Macleay 1000 off-road race in

July and he placed second by just 24 seconds to one of the Baker brothers in a purpose-built buggy.

As our Turbo Bluebird neared completion, a sister car to our Bluebird arrived from Japan. It had been built with many Australian components shipped to Japan and only required last-minute preparation before being ready to tackle The Mountain. What followed was a huge learning curve as our Datsun Rally Team were cast into the furnace and emerged as Nissan Sport. The Japanese crew, Hasemi and Hoshino, qualified outright 31st and quickest in the under 3-litre class. Fury was 43rd on the grid. Neither finished, let down by a gearbox at 66 laps and suspension failure at 30 laps respectively. But we were off and running!

*DNF, an abreviation of Did Not Finish, is used from herein. It reminds me of an oft used quote in this sport – "To finish first, first you must finish."

My story of these years can be found in the companion book – *Nissan Sport: Touring Car Racing in Australia.* Please get in touch to reserve a copy.

EARLY DAYS

1958 MOBILGAS ROUND AUSTRALIA TRIAL

As a crew member of Nissan Motor Co.'s first ever entry in an international rally, Datsun legend and stalwart Bruce Wilkinson must surely have felt some trepidation as he sat at the start line of the 1958 Mobilgas Round Australia Trial. He was the local navigator and jammed into the back seat of a Datsun 1000 – a tiny car in the league of an Austin A30. Christened 'Fuji-Go', this was the first of the Datsun 210s and used the company's first ever, over-head valve production engine! In the front seat were two Japanese nationals with very little English, Nanba san and Okuyama san.

This was the ninth long distance trial run in Australia so Bruce would have had some idea of the challenge ahead – 19 days covering more than 16,000 kms of mostly unsealed roads, clockwise around the driest continent in the world is not to be sneezed at, even in this day and age – back then it would have severely tested cars and all concerned.

Car #19 endured however and took the under 1000cc class win. A sister car (christened 'Sakura-Go') placed fourth in class. The Japanese returned home as heroes and were taken on a national tour standing in the back of a vehicle that looked as if it could have been their rally car with the

roof panel removed – an additional trial I'd imagine. Bruce, on the other hand, returned home with his memories and a lifetime friendship with the man who was to become President, Nissan Motorsport International Co. (Nismo) – Nanba San (Yasuhara Nanba).

Entering the event was the brainchild of Marketing Manager, Yutaka Katayama (later to be President of Nissan Motor Corp. U.S.A.) who had a strong belief that motorsport was the best way to build strength, endurance and performance into the Datsun brand – obviously a visionary. To crew 'Fuji', Yasuharu Nanba, then employed as a test driver, must have looked a likely candidate and it appears from a later interview that he embraced the idea and took joint ownership.

Fuji Go and crew battling sand

On the other hand, Yoshitane Oya, Manager, Inspection Department, Yokohama Plant, who must not have stepped back fast enough and got the lead driver's seat in 'Sakura', the sister car, is quoted in an interview: *"If you are ordered to do it, you have to do it."* And later: *"One way or another we managed it. Somehow we got to the finishing line."* And finally: *"I thought, we're saved! Now I don't have to drive anymore! I just didn't want to drive any more... that's how I felt."*

Needless to say it was a terrific beginning to Datsun/Nissan's career on the international rallying stage and would inspire many Datsun rally crews to follow. The car is now reverently displayed at Nissan's heritage museum at Zama in Japan.

As a fledgling motor company, such joy and satisfaction with a win in the tiny class was, I suppose, understandable. Aspirations for outright glory were still a way off but would develop as the company matured and its self esteem grew.

Eleven years later a team of Datsun 1600 SSSs broke the historic UK/Euro car stranglehold on world rallying, dominating the 1969 East African Safari, placing 1st, 2nd & 4th and rocketing the Datsun brand into the world rallying stratosphere. The winning crew of Herrmann Edgar/Hans Schuller were rewarded with an entry in the next major enduro, the 1970 Ampol Round Australia Trial.

A Datsun 1600 SSS evaluation vehicle, being used as a company car at the time by one of Nissan's execs, was requisitioned and given to Bruce Wilkinson to build up into a rally car. Initially, Nissan CEO in Australia, George Denner, asked Bruce to prepare the car so that it would not require a service crew!! George was quickly convinced that what he was asking was impossible for such a gruelling event. Bruce, together with his Service Manager Randall Cooke, had just two weeks to prepare the car. Bruce sacrificed his own entry with navigator Ian Inglis, to be a competitive service crew – arguably an even more gruelling task.

The full story of the event is very well covered by Jeff Cameron with considerable input from Bruce Wilkinson, in Volume 28 No. 3 (Winter 2020), of the HRA News which should be available at https://hra.org.au. Spoiler alert: The Herrmann/Schuller 1600 SSS placed equal first with French team Jean-Claude Ogier and his wife Lucette in one of three DS21 Citroëns. Other makers entering teams included Holden, Ford, Renault and Mitsubishi!

Other than the spectacular launch of the 240Z and it winning the 1971 East African Safari (Herrmann/Schuller again), not a great deal of detail is available to support other recorded Datsun rally successes between 1959 and 1972.

Until the mid sixties, rallies were either 'trials', where the aim was mostly to endure a long arduous course, or navigational challenges, where the aim was to interpret convoluted instructions, plot points on maps, and then follow the calculated route successfully. Timing (by various means) was used to split those who were able to follow the intended route without fault.

At about this time, top level rallies in Australia evolved to include speed events where the aim was to be the fastest crew over the prescribed, but secret, sections of the route. Accurate and straightforward instructions were provided to make it much easier for cars to follow the correct route. Timing was initially recorded to the minute but soon advanced to the quarter minute and later to the second as the competition developed.

These events were almost exclusively conducted at night as they were largely run on what was, strictly speaking, public roads and tracks (headlights would show approaching vehicles). As they were also mostly conducted in forests away from built up areas, it was also unlikely that non-rally vehicles would be in the area.

Later, the top level of rallies would evolve further to what is known as 'pace-noted' events where the route is published beforehand and be available for practising and 'note' taking. These are now almost always conducted in daylight and held on roads closed to the public.

Apart from minor class results in the 1962 and 1964 BP Rallies of South Eastern Australia with Cedric 1900s, Datsun rally successes began in earnest in Australia with Datsun 1000s in 1967 and were soon followed by the incredible success of the Datsun 1600, beginning in 1968 (when it was first released here) and continuing to this day.

1972

In 1972, possibly in response to Mitsubishi's success at the 1971 Southern Cross International Rally, Nissan began sending Japanese 'works' prepared Datsuns to Australia on 'carnets'[1] and this signalled the beginning of the era covered in this book.

Prior to the 1972 Southern Cross there had been only a smattering of minor placings in the first three rounds of the Australian Rally Championship events, mostly due to the efforts of Peter Lang in his 1600, a hot-shot of this era. At the Warana Rally (ARC Round 4 in Queensland) Bruce Wilkinson, Manager of the Australian Datsun Rally team, entered himself, as a shakedown for the 'Cross' (as it had become fondly known), in a 'works' development 180B SSS. This car featured a very early version of an electronic engine management system (then abbreviated to ECGI) but it was not happy. It did not feature in the results of the Warana (Car #5) or the Cross (Car #8) and Bruce does not remember the ECGI fondly, in fact at the car's next outing, the BP Rally of 1973 for Gil Davis and Peter Haas, the fuel injection had been abandoned for the usual Solex side-draft carburettors. Bruce had pointed out all the ECGI components sitting unloved on a bench at Hartwell Datsun when he was showing me around in 1975.

Team boss Wilkinson shake-down for 1972 Southern Cross in ECGI 610 SSS

Datsun's success in ARC events would soon change though, with 'works' cars remaining in the country after the Cross being very competitive – in coming years Datsun would dominate this highest level of the sport in our country.

So, for the 1972 Southern Cross, Nissan entered an East African Safari spec 240Z for Rauno Aaltonen/Steve Halloran and works 180B SSSs for Edgar Herrmann/Mike Mitchell and Bruce Wilkinson/Roger Bonhomme. They also sent several Japanese mechanics and a Team

---

1. A Carnet is a Visa type of document for a car. The document describes the vehicle including body and engine numbers, the owner, Nissan Motor Co. in our case, and states the period of time the vehicle can stay in the country – after which it must leave or the appropriate import duty paid. Many rally cars were instead crushed under customs supervision. The Datsun Rally Team cars carried carnet plates in place of registration plates and these plate numbers were commonly used to identify them.

Manager to prepare, service and maintain the cars. This was when we first met Mabo Kobayashi and Gun Kobayashi, two talented rally mechanics we were delighted to welcome back for several more 'Crosses.

A Datsun 1600 was privately entered by a B. Wilkinson for the pairing of Yoshio Iwashita/T. Gotoh as Car 16. It was acquisitioned from the Datsun Sales Centre used car lot and rapidly prepared at Bruce Wilkinson Motors – no doubt using many works bits, so we could probably call it a works-supported car.

Car 6 on the entry list was a Datsun 1600 for Peter Lang/E. O'Cleary and entered by Gerry Ball Tuning, a name that will feature prominently later. Five additional privately entered 1600s and one 180B SSS were cars 19, 29, 38, 46, 48 & 55 being driven by R. Johnson, Bruce Cheeseman (610), Arthur Jackson, Helmut Goetz, R. Longmore and E. Bell.

The 'Cross was returning to the central coast of New South Wales for the third time but, for the first time, almost every competitor was supported by at least one 'service crew' vehicle. It turned out to be the most fiercely fought Southern Cross to that time, with a high percentage of its total distance being competitive and several of those competitive sections being longer than had been set before.

Aaltonen in the 240Z set the pace from the first competitive section and 'clean-sheeted' (meaning to beat the assigned time for the section and losing no points) despite completing the last 10kms with a flat tyre!

Aaltonen / Halloran 1972 Southern Cross Rally – Z rear ends were problematic but they managed 2nd place.

According to the organiser of the event, Dan White, *"Rauno lead the event at the end of the first night but Halloran missed a 'call' early on the next division allowing Cowan's and Chivas' Mitsubishi Galants through into 1st and 2nd places. Aaltonen recovered well but never headed Cowan again for the event. The two new Galant GTOs of Chivas and Stewart were in the process of homologation and, following Nissan's post event protest, they were not included in the final results. There was a counter protest lodged by Mitsubishi against advertising above the window line of the Datsuns but this was regarded as a frivolous protest and rightly dismissed by the event stewards."* So the mood between these fierce rivals was set.

Datsuns featured strongly in the results with Aaltonen/Halloran second and Herrmann/Mitchell fourth, but a disappointing result when compared with Mitsubishi's first and third. It was to become a theme as Andrew Cowan had won the first of what was to become four straight wins for both himself and Mitsubishi.

The privately entered Datsun 1600s of Jackson/Godden (car 38) and Goetz/McFadzean (car 46) finished fifth and tenth, giving Datsun four of the top ten.

1972 Australian Championship event successes for Datsun were almost zero, saved only by Helmut Goetz/Mike Mitchell's equal sixth place with Gil Davis' XU1, the only placing in the 49th Anniversary Alpine Rally.

After the Southern Cross Edgar Herrmann stayed on and teamed with Roger Bonhomme to run the last significant event for the year, the Dulux Rally in Rauno Aaltonen's 240Z. Interestingly, the Herrmann/Mitchell Southern Cross 180B SSS was entered for Datsun Racing Team boss John Roxburgh and Mike Mitchell – one of Roxburgh's very few outings in a rally car. They didn't feature in the results.

Datsun Racing Team boss having a go in the dirt

Roger Bonhomme has generously provided me a story of his recollections of the era and the drivers he teamed with for this book and this seems an appropriate place for it. Thanks Roger.

RECOLLECTIONS OF A DATSUN NAVIGATOR

It seems to me that Japanese car manufacturers have had a love affair with Australian rallying. Perhaps it's because Australia is so different from Japan – the wide open spaces, heat, dust, an empty remoteness inhabited by strange and often nasty animals.

Datsun dabbled with our bigger events from the 1958 Mobilgas Round Australia Trial. But it was the Southern Cross Rallies held between 1966 and 1980 that really grabbed the interests of the Japanese, particularly Datsun-Nissan and Mitsubishi. Other

Japanese car makers, such as Subaru, also put their toes into the water briefly.

I was involved as a navigator with the Datsun-Nissan Rally Team at the height of the annual Southern Cross Rally battles between Datsun and Mitsubishi. Every October each manufacturer imported its latest rally weapons in teams of two to five rally cars, supported by well equipped service personnel and, often, team managers. The world's best rally drivers were employed to fling these cars through the generally dusty and unforgiving forests in northern NSW.

No stone was left unturned by Datsun-Nissan and Mitsubishi to take rally honours. There was absolutely no doubt that winning a Cross was very, very important indeed. The winning car was flown (complete with genuine rally mud, dust and lolly wrappers) to the Tokyo Motor Show where it took pride of place in the winning manufacturer's stand. The plans of the Japanese were made a lot harder by Ford Motor Company (UK) who often entered the latest of their Escort rocketships piloted by rally gods such as Vatanen, Clark, Makinen, Mikkola and Waldegard with support from local heroes Carr and Bond.

Herrmann & Bonhomme Car #3 in the '72 Dulux Rally.

My entry into this high powered, squillion dollar world of rallying came in 1972 when the Australian manager of the Datsun-Nissan Rally team, Bruce Wilkinson, asked me to navigate for him in a team 180B SSS. Although I had, at that stage in my career, navigated for several factory teams (Renault, BLMC and Holden) nothing prepared me for the sheer effort that Datsun-Nissan put into winning a Southern Cross Rally. We had umpteen team meetings, service crews comprising both Japanese and Australian mechanics went through servicing drills, we navigators learned myriad mechanical things including the intricacies of swapping the wiring looms of our cars should the original fail.

For Bruce and me it was all a bit anti-climactic. Our SSS was fitted with an experimental fuel injection system and it still needed a bit of sorting. It was very important to the team that we finish so cross country navigating to stay inside late running time was the order of my workdays (or, rather, nights).

A month later the team employed me to compete in the Dulux Rally, navigating East African Safari winner Edgar Herrmann in a powerful 240Z. The Dulux was an unusual event, comprising conventional rally sections, circuit races and hill climbs. I even got to drive a couple of races at the twisty Winton, Victoria, circuit. Although we were pretty fast, we had to settle for third place as nothing could match the Holden Dealer Team's Torana XU-1s of Colin Bond and Peter Brock. In 1970 Edgar had become well known to local rally fans by finishing equal first with co-driver Hans Schuller in the Ampol Trial, a 10,000km slog around eastern and central Australia. They drove a Datsun 1600 SSS.

For 1973 I rejoined the team to navigate in the 'Cross for a second Safari winner, Shekhar Mehta. That year the heavens opened up, giving us the wettest event on record. The rain decimated the field and only seven cars were classified as finishers. Our 240Z was not one of them. Several sections in the event were over 100km long, necessitating in-stage refuelling and servicing (in your own time, of course). A side effect of these huge stages was the craving of smokers. So yes, I had to light up a couple of smokes for my chauffeur mid-stage. Most unusual! I have to say, as a smoker myself (then), that he drove and smoked very well one-handed.

As multiple Safari winners, Edgar and Shekhar were obviously very quick punters. They both had that rare ability to stroke their cars along at very high speed over the roughest of terrain. However, despite their undoubted talents, the next rally driver I sat alongside for Nissan in the Southern Cross would have blown them into the weeds. Meet Harry Källström, a tubby, slow moving Swede with a straggly moustache. He certainly didn't look like a rally driver, but he was the fastest man I ever enjoyed sitting alongside.

For three years, we partnered to drive Datsun's then current world rally car – the 710 Violet. Not released in Australia, the 710 looked like a slightly smaller 180B SSS. It was crammed full of Nissan's latest rally technology including two litre engines with either single or double overhead camshafts, close ratio five speed gearboxes and suspension components built to take rugged rally roads at top speeds.

Harry had wonderful car control – the ability to drift a rally car sideways through any corner. He accelerated the car hard everywhere – including downhill. He looked relaxed but his concentration over all sections, long and short, was complete. I remember only one small mistake. He got a little too sideways on one downhill slope and the car started to spin. Harry steered the car around in a tightening loop, selected first gear and away we went. I did learn a few more Swedish swear words though!

Despite his poor command of English, he concentrated fully on my instructions and we never over-shot an intersection or took a wrong turn. He was the complete professional, which is why he won the European Rally Championship and twice took off the prestigious RAC Rally in the UK during the early '70's.

Unfortunately, although I felt we were a very strong team in a competitive car, Harry and I never stood on the podium in our three events together. A broken lower control arm put us out in the first event and mechanical niggles during the other two dropped us well back.

The rally team was fully supported by excellent mechanics, both Japanese and Australian. They popped up at regular intervals to check our cars, fix problems, clean glass areas and send us on our way. They drove a fleet of heavily laden Nissan E20 vans between service points.

In 1975 Nissan had a new local star – George Fury. To increase his knowledge of the 710s, he was given Harry's ex-Cross car to run in the first round of the '75 Australian Rally Championship, the Mazda House 1000 Rally. It came complete with me as navigator. We had a smooth, trouble-free run and ended up with the big cigar. I remember that during the event, George fiddled almost constantly with the car's adjustable braking system. It had an under-dash control which changed braking bias from front to rear. I got the feeling that George couldn't find a balance that suited him so he put it halfway and left it there! Nissan's move to sign up George paid off handsomely. He was always competitive in the last few Crosses and, with long time navigator Monty Suffern, won in 1978 and 1979.

So what's it like being a "works" navigator? During my 25 years in motor sport I drove or navigated in 14 different models for nine manufacturers or distributors. So I know what it's all about.

Competing for Datsun-Nissan during the early 1970's was certainly one of the most enjoyable times of my career and I took the work very seriously. I read the regulations, spoke to the mechanics about components I might repair or replace mid-section, stayed off the booze and checked out the opposition. During events, I realised that, in most cases, I was the 'local' and tried to help my driver as much as possible with simple, explicit instructions not only on the special stages but also on transport sections through towns and other traffic-congested areas. I spent a lot of time meticulously reading route instructions for each stage, using a Texta to underline consecutive instructions that were close together.

A good navigator has to sit in a car whilst it is being driven at unbelievable speeds over unforgiving terrain. He or she must concentrate to the highest degree to give the driver a constant flow of clear, accurate information. The voice must not quiver from excitement or fear. The navigator has to be supremely organised, calm and confident at all times, despite any number of outside pressures. A navigator must be able to sit without emotion in an artificial cocoon whilst the rest of the world goes mad around him.

Harry Källström with Roger Bonhomme Car #2 for the 1974 'Cross

No it isn't easy. But if you get it right, then rallying can be a wonderful, rewarding sport.

1973

By 1973 Datsuns were beginning to show up in podium positions in Australian Rally Championship events, despite Holden's Torana XU1s generally dominating.

In round one, The Southern 500 Rally in South Australia, for example, the works 240Z of Frank Kilfoyle/Mike Osborne finished sixth and then, while looking good in round two, The Classic Rally in South Gippsland, Vic, failed to finish due to differential failure. They followed up with a good equal second to the McLeod/Mortimer XU1 in round three, The Bunbury Curran Rally in New South Wales. In round four, The Bega Valley Rally (renamed this year from the Snowy Mountains Rally) the Kilfoyle/Osborne 240Z led for most of the event but again DNF'd with diff failure. The Datsun team didn't venture north to Queensland for The Warana Rally, round five in '73, so representation fell to Bryan Evans/Barry Lake who placed fifth in their non-works 240Z.

The sixth and final round of the ARC this year was incorporated in the Victorian classic, The Alpine Rally in North Eastern Victoria, this year its 50th anniversary and known as the Golden Alpine. Everything came together for Datsun and the Kilfoyle/Osborne team. Maybe due to a lack of spare 240Z diffs they ran the red works 180B SSS which had recently done the BP Rally of SE Australia for Davis/Haas. Running in the 'Open' class, Kilf and Osborne dominated The Alpine and won convincingly, although not eligible for ARC points due to the event's regulations. Also not eligible for points and running in the 'Open' category was a certain George Fury and Monty Suffern who were fast and consistent in George's now 2-litre Mk I Cortina and who were rewarded with fourth place outright.

Vic Hughes photo

Frank Kilfoyle & Mike Osborne, '73 Repco Alpine Rally

Frank Kilfoyle and Mike Osborne ended the ARC year equal seventh in the Drivers' and Navigators Championships but would have been much higher placed had they been able to claim points for The Alpine win.

For myself, October 1973 must have been excitedly anticipated as mate, Chris Power and I had a grand tour planned. We were taking in the Bathurst 1000 (this year upgraded from 500 miles) and then cruising on to Sydney and Port Macquarie for our first experience of:

The Southern Cross International Rally.

Maybe the plan was to help service for Bruce Wilson/Bill Granger (whom I'd been supporting in events in Victoria) in a 180B SSS, Car #34, entered by Datsun Distribution P/L – but I'm guessing a bit here. George Fury/Monty Sufferen were starting right behind them as Car #35 so that must have become interesting not long into the event.

I remember nothing of the Bathurst 1000 now but records show it was won by Alan Moffat and Ian Geoghegan in a Ford XA Falcon in front of Brock/Chivas in a GTR XU1 Torana. They were followed home by Colin Bond and Leo Geoghegan in another XU1, Bob Jane and John Harvey in another and Bob Forbes and Dick Johnson in yet another. Moffat sure rained on the Holden parade that year. I'm sure I would have been much more interested though in Bill Evans and James Laing -Peach dominating Class A in the Datsun Racing Team's 1200 Coupe!

When we arrived in Sydney for the Cross, that parade was being rained on too, and the rain didn't stop for the whole four days. It became known as the 'wet one'.

The green Kilfoyle/Osborne 180B SSS at service stop

Nissan were now beginning to get serious and had entered works prepared 240Zs for Tony Fall/Steve Halloran, Car #1, Shehkar Mehta/Roger Bonhomme, Car #2, and Bob Watson/Jeff Beaumont, Car #17. They also entered an uncharacteristically lime green-coloured 180B SSS (TKS56 SE 3240) for Frank Kilfoyle/Mike Osborne, Car #8, and a locally-built blue one for Fury/Suffern, Car #35.

Re the blue 180B SSS, Monty says: *"... it was originally for Gil to prepare and drive in the 1973 Cross. He asked me to navigate for him, and when Gil had to drop out I suggested to Bruce that George finish the preparation and have the drive. George immediately* took several weeks off work and set about it. The performance in the 1973 event was sufficiently impressive, despite not finishing (halfway through the 3rd night), that the relationship continued. Bruce knew he'd found a good team."

Somewhat mysteriously the 1972 Herrmann/Mitchell Works 180B SSS was entered as Car #26 for Chris Murray/Dean Eckert by Datsun Distribution P/L. SA How DDSA got control of that car and how Chris Murray earned the right to drive it remains a mystery to me. Datsun Distribution P/L Vic. entered a near standard one for Bruce Wilson/ Bill Granger, Car #34, and one of the remaining four, privately entered 180B SSSs, was Car #41, entered and driven by Ross Dunkerton teamed with John Large. There were six private Datsun 1600s, and one Datsun 1200 for Bill Evans/Mike Mitchell, Car #28, Bill planning to back up his Bathurst class win.

Bob Watson & Jeff Beaumont slip-sliding to 8th o'right in '73 Cross

Surely this was a line-up that could get the job done for Nissan.

Other names that will still be meaningful to Datsun rally fans all these years later included, Stewart McLeod in an XU1– Car #5, Greg Carr in a Holden Kingswood – Car #38, and Colin Bond, starting last car due to an eligibility dispute, in an XU1, as Car #74. And many more, a veritable who's who of rallying including, of course, a team of five Mitsubishi entered Lancer GSRs with their own list of stars, all lined up to make this the most memorable rallying event in Australia's history. But it poured – and the event was memorable for other things – mud and river crossings and boggings and impassable hills.

Remembered by Peter Otzen: *At pre-event scrutineering, the Kilfoyle/Osborne works 180B SSS recorded a sound level reading of 108dBA and was threatened with exclusion. The Nissan team quickly sourced and fitted a downward-facing tail pipe which allowed the car to scrape under the limit.*

Anyway, we all got thoroughly wet and muddy, Tony Fall rolled his

240Zs and Shekhar Mehta damaged his Z's read end and both retired early, everyone who could, battled on as well they were able, all to see Mitsubishi Lancer GSRs take first, second, third, and fourth places. The best Datsun could salvage was a sixth for Kilfoyle/Osborne in the green 180B SSS, eighth for Watson/Beaumont in a LHD works 240Z, and yes, Evans/Mitchell dominated their class and came tenth outright. A relatively unknown (in the Eastern states) Ross Dunkerton/John Large, Car #41, struggled home in Ross' 180B SSS to finish eleventh. I'm sure many other horror stories are still buried in the mud around Port Macquarie but Dunkerton's seems to have survived, even though rather well-worn.

Bill Evans and Mike Mitchell – happy to have endured and won their class in the '73 'Cross

1973 was my first attack on the Southern Cross. The event was run in horrific weather conditions and many roads became impassable. My most vivid memory of that year was tackling a very steep hill at night in my standard 180B SSS. Cars were bogged all over the hill. With pedal to the floor, I managed to pass all but one of them, a Mitsubishi Galant. The car behind me decided to have one more try and edged a bumper in front of us.

As it was obvious none of us were going anywhere, all three drivers decided to negotiate our way out. We agreed to assist each other over the crest. We would push the first car, then all push the second and so on. With much grunting and groaning the six crew members from the three front cars pushed the Galant over the crest, but once freed they disappeared into the night! With only four people left to push the remaining two cars, we managed to get the Mazda over the crest. This time the competitor returned as agreed, but our Datsun was too firmly stuck for just the four of us, who were now exhausted.

Eventually we did get out by going back down the hill but it was a continuous grind to the finish. In fact, I remember one stage was so slippery my car started to slide backwards off a cliff, when the handbrake wouldn't hold it. I had to jump out and lay under the back

wheel to stop it sliding into the ravine. Such are the recollections of my first Southern Cross and what I took away from it was – never rely on another competitor to get you to the end, and no matter how bad you think the weather is, it can always get worse.

Two Datsun related stories from Tom Snooks' account in his '*History of the Southern Cross Rally*' were from the first night's run from Sydney to Port Macquarie:

"*Tony Fall in the 240Z put up a good performance but was hampered by repeated punctures. On one section he suffered two punctures, using both spares wheels, and was clattering along on the bare rim after a third when he came across teammate Frank Kilfoyle off the road in their Datsun 180B SSS. They swapped a tow back onto the road for a spare wheel and both continued on.*"

And, from the second night: "*The second division started in fine and warm conditions, but the roads were still greasy. Not long after the start Tony Fall came unstuck when his 240Z slid on a bridge, thumped a bank and then rolled. Cowan had spun into the inside bank on the same corner and the other Lancers nudged the outside bank. None were damaged.*"

My own memories of the 1973 'Cross include hanging around at service points with the Datsun team and at one stage overhearing a conversation between Mehta and Fall who apparently had a running tally of the 240Zs they'd rolled that year. I'm not sure if I chuckled along or if I was overcome with the sadness of it all, I think I even had a sneaking suspicion that the two of them conspired to find an early exit from an unpleasant event, but surely champions don't think like that… The spectating was miserable as the survivors battled the elements to get to the finish. I imagine I was reasonably glad to get home from our big adventure.

1974

My abbreviated and Datsun-focussed reports of the ARC Series from 1974 to 1981 and the Southern Cross Rallies from 1973 to 1980 draw significantly from Tom Snooks' *'History of the Australian Rally Championship 1968-1988'*, and also his *'Southern Cross International Rally 1966-1980, A History of the Events'*. For a more comprehensive review I encourage you to seek out your own copies of these fine works.

The 1974 Australian Rally Championship was again convincingly dominated by Torana GTR XU1s, winning five of the seven rounds and coming second in the other two! Peter Lang, with George Shepheard calling the way, steered to victory in the opening round, **The Semperit 1600** in WA with Stewart McLeod/Adrian Mortimer placing second in their privately run 260Z.

Ross Dunkerton/John Large would not have been all that happy about fifth place in Ross' 240Z in their home state round – and having four 'Eastern Staters' including arch rival of the time, Stewart McLeod in a similar car, in front of them would have put salt in that wound.

Colin Bond then teamed with George Shepheard to pretty much dominate the rest of the series.

A partly daylight-run, 'special stage' rally was conceived, organised and run in the forests around Canberra in late March 1974. **The Don Capasco Rally** was to be a trend setter and many similar events were organised in Australia from then on. George Fury ran his blue 180B SSS (Car 8) and placed fifth. It was to be George's last event in this car – he sold it to John Armitage when it became apparent he would be driving factory cars from then on. The McLeod/Mortimer 260Z placed second to Bob Watson/Jeff Beaumont in the exotic, Renault Australia loaned, Alpine A110. Greg Carr began his rise to domination of the Canberra rally with a sixth place in a Gerry

George & Monty in the blue, Aussie-built 180B SSS busy coming 5th in the Don Capasco.

Ball Tuning Datsun 1600, although he was 20 minutes behind Fury in fifth. See full report on this innovative event here: https://www.archives.act.gov.au/find_of_the_month/2018/november/previous-find-of-the-month-112018

Datsun did better in Round 2, The Akademos Rally in Victoria, with Dunkerton/Large making the trip across the country and claiming second place in their 240Z, narrowly beating the SA team, McLeod/Mortimer (260Z). Bill Evans/Mike Mitchell backed them up well placing fifth in their 120Y.

Round 3, The Bega Rally, NSW saw Zs going one better with McLeod winning and Dunkerton settling for third, followed impressively by Bill Evans/Mike Mitchell in their 120Y! A 1600 of Cheeseman and Lockie a way back in fifth place.

Round 4, The Uniroyal Southern Rally in SA saw Dunkerton/Large place third to the Bond/Shepheard XU1 and Dean Rainsford/Graham West in a Porsche 911S second. The Evans/Mitchell mighty 120Y was fifth edging out the McLeod/Mortimer 260Z.

Round 5, The Warana Rally in Queensland, was notable for being one of the few national events of this era where Dunkerton and Large didn't get to stand on the podium – an altercation with a tree and subsequent repairs saw them missing some stages. It mattered not, Bond/Shepheard pretty much had a mortgage on the championship by then. When done and dusted it was they who'd

Dunko and John Large in the 240Z sans bonnet after a collision with a Qld. tree.

won again with McLeod/Mortimer runners up, three minutes back. Bill Evans had coaxed the little 120Y into fourth, narrowly beating locals Murray Coote and Brian Marsden in their 1200.

Round 6, The Bunbury Curran Rally in NSW, provided another win for the Bond/Shepheard XU1. Second was McLeod/Mortimer in the 260Z and third, with their best result of the season, was the Evans/Mitchell 120Y. This must have been an 'interesting' event as third and fourth were almost an hour behind second with fifth a further three hours back.

Following the Southern Cross International, The Alpine Rally in Victoria finalised the championship and saw McLeod/Mortimer in the 260Z managing to just pip the Bond/Shepheard XU1. The no-doubt-rather-tired 180B SSS that Kilfoyle had won the 1973 Alpine with, was entered again for Kilfoyle/Osborne but it did not feature in the results and this proved to be its last event. The next best Datsun was the Pike/Cardi 180B an hour back in sixth place.

Bill Evans was fifth in the Drivers' Championship in 1974, an astounding effort in a mostly standard 120Y. Colin Bond won again with 45 points with Stewart McLeod second on 36 points and Ross Dunkerton third on 16 points. He would do better the following year though, and the next one after that, and the one after that, and only slightly less well in the three years after that!! Always in a Datsun.

The Southern Cross International Rally

The '74 Cross attracted an entry list only slightly less impressive that the previous year. Mitsubishi entered three new Lancers for Cowan, Singh and Stewart, and three 1973 model Lancers for Ferguson, Chivas and Riley. Nissan entered a pair of new 710 SSSs for Källström (LZ18 twin cam engine) and Kilfoyle (LR18 single cam engine) and the green (but now painted blue with red and white stripes) 1972 Southern Cross 180B SSS (LR18 single cam) for Fury/Suffern. Iwashita entered another 710 SSS with factory support.

The full entry list of 64 cars and crews can be studied at http://southerncrossrally.blogspot.com/2014/01/1974-list-of-entries.html

Renault entered Bob Watson in the Alpine A110 Coupe in which he'd won the Don Capasco Rally earlier in the year. It proved to be somewhat unsuitable for such an arduous event.

Källström and Bonhomme on day 1 of the '74 'Cross

The Datsun team got off to a less than illustrious start when Kilfoyle/Richards flipped their 710 and retired in the second competitive section. McLeod/Mortimer in the 240Z also had a short event – a fire causing their early retirement. At the end of the night though, with

Källström and Cowan level pegging on 43 and Fury next best on 50, things were actually looking pretty good.

In the first section on day two though, disaster struck again as Källström's 710 suffered suspension failure and could not continue. Many other crews ran out of their late time allowance when a slippery hill caught some out and a roadblock resulted. Only 16 crews were able to complete day two within allowable time.

The first of Kilf's two Datsun career-ending crashes.

Day three saw Fury/Suffern working hard at pegging back Cowan/Bryson but at night's end they'd been passed by Ferguson and Adcock who'd been quick and had had a clean run. There were six further retirements.

Just transporting through the Bellinger River crossing at Gordonville in 1974.

So day four began with just 10 starters. Cowan/Bryson on just 209 points cruised through to yet another fine victory followed by Singh/Connelly on 272 to make it a magnificent quinella for Mitsubishi. Fury/Suffern fought on doggedly in the 180B to gain a well deserved fourth on 1051 points after nearly missing out when George clobbered a bank and they needed to skip a few sections. Iwashita/Yasuoka in their semi-private 710 SSS helped make the results board look a little better for Datsun, coming in fifth on 2021 points and Victorians John Munro and Wal Harris brought their 1600 home as the last finisher in seventh place. An arduous event indeed with just seven finishers – they would become known as The Magnificent Seven.

Later in October, George and Monty used the 710 that had let Harry Källström down in the Cross, to win The RACV 500 in the Latrobe Valley, forerunner to the Holden Dealers 500.

1975

Early in '75 Wilkinson received a 710 SSS from Japan for testing and development. This was the first time the LZ DOHC engine was seen in Australia. It also arrived with the Nissan ECGI electronic fuel injection and ignition system but, following Bruce's experience with this in '74, and noting it hadn't improved much since, he soon removed the system and fitted the familiar Mikuni Solex carburettors.

The 1975 Australian Rally Championship quite clearly marked the transition from Holden to Datsun domination at that level of rallying in Australia.

Round 1, The Mazda House 1000 in NSW, was George Fury's first ARC round win. It was also the first ARC win for the Datsun Rally Team and the first time a Datsun 710 ran in the ARC. Less inevitably, it was also the first of very few times someone other than Monty Suffern pointed George the way, with Roger Bonhomme getting that gig. Dunkerton/Large, now with a 260Z and showing the Channel 9 sponsorship that would become a recognisable feature, ended the event equal second with Doug Stewart/Brian Hope in a Lancer although shortly after the halfway break Dunko surged past Fury to take the lead initiating one of their classic battles. Fury responded well and strung together a series of quickest times near the finish to take the win.

George Fury's first ARC win was with Roger Bonhomme!

Upgraded to a 260Z but still privateers, Dunkerton/Large then comfortably won Round 2, The Toms Tyres 1600, in perfect conditions in their home state of WA. Second and third places were also secured in 260Zs: locals John Edwards/Bill Philip and South Australians Stewart McLeod/Adrian Mortimer consecutively.

A mate and I drove my blue 1600 across the as-yet not fully sealed Nullabor as a grand adventure and to witness this event. My memory is far from crystal clear but as we left Melbourne I was only vaguely aware of Ross Dunkerton. By the time we turned for home, though, he'd joined my pantheon of heroes and we'd become friends. We journeyed down to his hometown of Narrogin, visited his Datsun dealerships, there and at Katanning, and went Marron fishing on the Buchanan River – brilliant!

The third major event of the year was the second running of The Don Capasco Rally in Canberra. Datsun apparently decided to use this event to gain some media attention as the only works Datsun entered was for TV presenter and novice rally driver Peter Wherrett, with John Bryson navigating. The 'green' 180B SSS had been repainted blue with red roof and white side stripes for this event with a much wider than usual white stripe at the rear quarter panel area to accommodate the 'Torque' signage in large letters, this being the name of Wherrett's weekly national TV program for the ABC. The footage captured of the event was made into an episode.

Wherrett/Bryson 610 Torque-mobile proceeding well.

His service crew for the event included Frank Kilfoyle and John Bosua, two extensively experienced Datsun campaigners. The winner of the event was Greg Carr/Wayne Gregson in a Datsun 1600 prepared by Gerry Ball Tuning, second was Stewart McLeod/Adrian Mortimer, 260Z and third, Dean Rainsford/Rob Hunt in a Porsche 911. Wherrett did quite well to finish tenth with the car intact. This was to prove the 'green' car's last finish.

The Akademos, on May 25, was the third ARC round for '75 and it continued the trend of furious competition among the top contenders – 260Zs of Dunkerton/Large and McLeod/Mortimer, Fury/Suffern (first event in the recently arrived DOHC 710 SSS), and Kilfoyle, this time with Geoff Boyd navigating, in

Last hurrah for the 'green car'. Kilf/Boyd '75 Akademos

the blue-sided, but green underneath, 610 SSS.

Nearing the division break both Fury and Kilfoyle went straight on at a via point instead of turning left. This cost Kilf two minutes but Fury 15, so that at the division break, Fury/Suffern were placed sixth, 7 and 8 minutes behind Kilf and Dunko.

Mid division, following several punctures and other misadventures, Kilf, McLeod and Dunkerton were neck and neck for several stages until Kilf was able to pull one minute gap and it looked apparent that the ageing 180B SSS would triumph. It was not to be though as just 2 kms from the end of the last stage, Kilf was caught out by a tricky corner and ended the car's life against a tree. It was to be Kilf's last Datsun drive.

McLeod/Mortimer were awarded first place on 48 points and Dunkerton/Large second on 50 with Fury/Suffern having recovered most of what they'd lost from their wrong slot earlier to grab third with 55.

Dunkerton/Large subsequently protested regarding the allowance of two minutes to McLeod/Mortimer while they changed a wheel in control (the first ever protest at an Akademos) meaning that McLeod and Dunkerton were awarded equal first placings.

The Howard Marsden entered BDA Escort for Watson/Beaumont placed fourth, 3 minutes behind George and Monty. This event was hard fought at a fast and furious pace and it seemed rallying in Australia had really stepped up a notch.

Fourth round of the ARC in '75 was The Bega Valley Rally in SE New South Wales on the June long weekend. It proved a hard fought and controversial event with Fury/Suffern leading at the end of the first night but retiring with a collapsed rear end early on the second. Dunkerton battled hard with the Holdens of Bond/Shepheard and the Jackson brothers but the Bega favours horsepower and he narrowly succumbed to them both, finishing third (eventually, after protests and counter protests were held and decided.)

The Warana Rally in Queensland was the fifth round in '75 and all the championship front runners were there in a field of 52. Bond/Shepheard were quick out of the blocks but gearbox trouble forced their retirement soon afterward. This left the 260Zs of Dunkerton/Large and McLeod/Mortimer to battle it out – pressure being applied from behind by the Mulligan/Gocentas Torana L34. Among the arduous string of stages the event had one exceeding 100 kms, a rarity by then for an ARC round. Bob Watson/Jeff Beaumont in the Escort were fastest on this one showing that Bob still had what it took to be competitive.

Watson/Beaumont eventually finished third to the two 260Zs but were not eligible for ARC points. Dunkerton/Large defeated McLeod/Mortimer by a single minute giving the former crew an almost unassailable lead in the championship.

Dunko narrowly beats McLeod in the 1975 Warana

Round six for the year was The Walker Trophy Rally of SA. It was apparent that full minute scoring was too blunt an instrument and accordingly the Walker Trophy was the first ARC round to feature ¼ minute scoring. It was again a battle of the 260Zs with one more, locals Pike/Middleton, added for extra fun but we can't forget the other local crew of Rainsford/West in the Porsche 911 because they won the event by one quarter of a minute!

Both McLeod and Dunkerton spoiled their chances of winning with an off each, Dunkerton also running out of fuel but luckily where it cost them little time. In the end Dunkerton/Large were second, McLeod/Mortimer third and Pike/Middleton fourth – the Porsche spoiling a 260Z trifecta. Dunkerton/Large had scored well enough to lock up the 1975 Australian Rally Championship win for driver and navigator.

Ken Cusack photo

Early testing with one of the new 710s for '75 – no way of knowing whether George's, Rauno's or Harry's, but behind it lurks Harry's '74 SCR car in which George had recently won the ANZ Bank Mazda House Rally with Roger Bonhomme. Strange to see the new car without signage and decals. I can I.D. two of the watchers, far left and far right – can anyone improve on that?

The Southern Cross International Rally

Three pristine looking white twin cam 710s arrived at Wilkinson Motors around September in 1975.

Richard Power, (elder brother of my mate Chris) worked in Nissan's Marketing Department at the time. He was keenly interested in rallying and had an artistic flair and talent for design. I'll leave it to him to tell you his thoughts on the works cars' livery up until that time, and his concept for a makeover:

"The works cars which came here for the 1972 and 1973 Southern Cross Rallies were a darkish red with matt black hoods and a fairly thin white side stripe and signage lettering. When the team switched to 710s, I thought the existing livery was a perfunctory effort and was too indistinguishable in night rallying for both media and spectators.

The 710 SSS, like the 180B SSS, with its high windowsills, overdone overhangs, fussy sculpturing and deep slab sides was a retrograde styling look compared to in-house designer, Teruo Uchino's lean, ageless, internationalist 510/1600.

Richard Power photo
Looking pristine in new colours fresh from H&H Panels, Burwood

The 710 needed new warpaint to do justice to a new but already successful brand in the increasingly designer world of big sponsor motorsport hero cars. Hence my offer to design something to disguise its unlovely lines.

I used Nissan's true corporate logo colours – a lighter red for the roof and, being a coupé, the boot-lid, pale blue hood and 'beltline' flashes along each upper side, with signage reversed in white, and the main side areas white, providing an uninterrupted sweep front to rear and avoiding a stuck-on look for official rally ID/number boards and other sponsor decals, and to emphasise the wheel arch flares. As a nod to the purists, the blue bonnet was matt-finished to cut reflection from our southern hemisphere, clear-sky moonshine, or maybe I'd had too much thereof…

Grille apertures are always a big styling identifier so I highlighted the 710's 'mouth' with a broad white perimeter stripe bordered with thinner red and blue stripes which then ran down and along the sills and highlighted the outer edges of the wheel arch flares, all to further slim down the car's slab sides and present a finished look.

The factory essentially carried over my livery onto the Stanza when it replaced the 710 in 1978 but I didn't think it worked so well. The Stanza was an attempt to regain the simple elegance and elan of the 1600. By then though, I'd left NMA for Ford Australia."

The three cars were ferried around to H&H Panels (near Bruce's workshop) where Laurie Wilson applied Richard's concept. It would go on to become the 710's global rally livery.

My own involvement in preparation for the '75 Cross was again after hours, being given small jobs by Mabo San or Gun San which I imagine they would have thoroughly checked before they headed back to their accommodation late at night. I remember crawling under dashes and soldering in map lights and what not. They probably needed someone as small as themselves...

Everyone had high expectations and, assembled in a row, the 710s certainly looked ready to take on the world.

The Cross began well with Källström leading early and then Fury/Suffern leading by three minutes at the end of Div 1 at Port Macquarie. Cowan in a Mitsubishi Lancer was in second position, Greg Carr/Wayne Gregson placing third in the yellow Gerry Ball Tuning 180B SSS (the re-shelled works car Fury had driven to 4th O/R in the 1974 Southern Cross), and Källström/Bonhomme equal fourth with Hannu Mikkola's Lancer. Dunkerton/

When Harry met Roger things began well but ended in disaster.

Beaumont in the works 240Z had a coming together with a spectator on a transport section, likely still coming to grips with positioning the LHD car on the road. A rear wishbone was damaged and, as they had no spare, this forced their retirement.

Division 2 was a nightmare though, as first Aaltonen/Souminen's LZ18 self destructed, followed by Källström's and then finally Fury's as he was storming away at the front of the field with the dust-free run. Broken pistons, all three. It was left to Greg Carr/Wayne Gregson to carry the Datsun flag.

The rest of the event was a test of who could endure and stay out of trouble and in the end only 14 crews completed the full course – Carr/Gregson were third to two works Mitsubishi Lancers. Once again the Datsun team left Port Macquarie with tails between legs. All three blown engines were crated up and returned to Japan immediately post-event.

Monty wrote an article about this sorry saga which was sadly lost with a computer hard disk, but here's a snippet he remembers: *"...it was about the Cross where Harry's and Rauno's cars both blew up on the first couple of stages, and we managed to almost make it through the second night before we blew up too. The story was really about the bottle of "insurance" we carried in case of mishap, and how George was heard to call me a "weak bastard" when I only had a couple of swigs of the port, while he finished it off while we walked the 11 km (or something like that) to the next control in the cold, dark night."*

Fury hangs it all out for the cameras.

Immediately after the Cross we did the **Holden Dealers 500** (first event timed to the second in Victoria) in Gippsland. George and Monty (Car #1) used their Cross 710 after we'd fitted another engine and they placed second to the Bond/Shepheard L34 Torana by just 20 seconds.

The final round of the Australian Rally Championship for 1975 was **The Kleber Alpine Rally** but this year the championship had been decided months before the crews arrived and was something of an anti-climax from the ARC point of view. As usual though, it was a long, hot and tough event in traditional Alpine country in north east Victoria.

Dunko's works 240Z not looking its best.

In division one Dunkerton rolled the LHD works 240Z causing light all-over body damage but also bent suspension and it was not able to continue.

The Open class was won by Carr/Gregson by more than 20 mins in their yellow 180B SSS fresh (sic) from its third place in the Southern Cross.

Greg Carr & Wayne Gregson heading for a big '75 Alpine win, sadly not eligible for ARC points though.

McLeod/Mortimer in the SA Datsun supported 260Z took the points in the ARC category.

So the stage was set for my life to be turned upside down.

At that time I'd been employed for two or so years by the Datsun Service Centre (a subsidiary of N.M.A) as a Service Advisor, a job I'd been offered by a girlfriend's father who, as chance would have it, was the Used Car Manager of the Datsun Sales Centre (another part of the company).

For context, when I joined NMA, Head Office was on the corner of Victoria and Leicester Streets at the top end of Melbourne's CBD and new Datsuns as well as Nissan commercial vehicles were being sold from the ground floor of this building. The Datsun Service Centre together with the used car division was in a building immediately east of the huge flagpole on the big roundabout at the top of Elizabeth Street. It later became a Ford dealership. Shortly after the release of the 180B and 120Y, when Datsun sales were rapidly blossoming, the Service Centre had become cramped and urgently needed to grow. Nissan bought a large building in Sturt Street, South Melbourne, previously a Rootes service outlet and, late in '75, we began the move.

New Car Sales Manager at this time, Bruce Wilson, as well as Commercial Vehicle Sales Manager, Mark Holmes, New Car Salesman, Ian Swan, Used Car Sales Manager, Ted Anderson and New Car Buyer Liaison Officer, Helen Morgan (for whom I had a crush) were all rallying or involved – Bruce running in the VRC. As a young guy interested in motorsport, I was drawn in.

I was going to the Wilson's place in Wonga Park of an evening to help prepare his 1600 and then heading off at weekends to events with his service crew. The Swans were also in Wonga Park so there was fun to be had in Ian's garage as well – before I knew it I was in up to my eyebrows.

As I said in the introduction, sometime shortly after we moved to Sturt St., I was summoned to Nissan Vice President, Australia, Mr Sasamoto's office for reasons unknown. With my eyes getting ever wider he explained that the rally team was to be brought inside the company and would be run out of the Sturt Street premises (where he and I both worked). He said he thought I should be the full time mechanic. He said Harry Firth had been approached to take on the role of Team Manager and they were awaiting his decision. I think he said I could begin straight away as two rally cars were arriving by truck that afternoon. I think he walked me up to the back corner of the service department parking area and showed me the floorspace allocated, pointed to some unused parts bins and racking and said I could begin moving them to enclose the area. Sure enough, trucks arrived, rally cars, tyres and parts were unloaded and my playpen began to take shape.

A few days later (maybe a week) I was called back to the wood-panelled office and told that Harry Firth had declined but a certain Howard Marsden (who I was only very vaguely aware of at the time) had been contracted and would be starting in a few weeks. Sas must have been able to tell that I'd had no second thoughts about accepting his offer as I don't recall being asked. Was I blessed or what?

The next thing I knew I was back in Sas' office once again and being introduced my new boss – the delightful and very friendly Howard Marsden. He told me all the things I most wanted to hear at the time (something he turned out to be really good at) and I got back to the job inspired and excited for what was to come. I was soon to meet and get to work with my ultimate superheroes of the time, wonderful people one and all and one of the best times of my life.

So sad to leave Bruce behind but maybe new boss Howard, might bring better luck...

1976

My first year full-time! When we began the newly corporatised Datsun Rally Team in the back corner of the Datsun Service Centre's vehicle parking area in Sturt Street, South Melbourne, we had three Violet 710s to play with. Also Ross Dunkerton was leaving the LHD 240Z with us as Howard (no doubt at Sas's 'suggestion') had agreed we'd prepare and service it for the ARC in '76.

The 710s were Fury's '75 Cross car (white sides), the blue-sided

NEWS RELEASE From the Public Relations Office
Nissan Motor Co. (Australia) Pty. Ltd.,
210 Victoria Street, Melbourne, 3000.
Tel. 347 3222, Cables "Datsun", Telex No. AA30589.

Date 2nd February, 1976
Reference No. 008/76
From G.M. CURRIE

TOP TEAM MANAGER FOR NEW DATSUN WORKS RALLY CARS

Nissan-Australia, makers of Datsuns have appointed Mr. Howard Marsden as Manager of their recently formed Competitions Department.

The rallying Datsuns will compete under the title of Nissan Motor-Australia Team abbreviated to the N.M.A. Team. The Datsuns will contest all seven events counting for the 1976 National Rally Championship. It will also run in Australia's two international rallies, The Southern Cross International in October and the Castrol International in March.

The move to a factory team follows the victory of the Channel 9/Ansett sponsored Datsun 260Z of West Australian, Ross Dunkerton, in the 1975 Australian Rally Championship series.

Dunkerton and Datsun took last year's title from the Holden Dealer Team which had won it the previous four years in succession.

Another Datsun 260Z, in the hands of South Australian Stewart McLeod, was runner-up to Dunkerton.

Dunkerton, again with last year's sponsors, will back up Victorian George Fury, Nissan-Australia's contracted driver, in the Datsun challenge for National rallying supremacy for 1976.

> Fury will compete in a Datsun 710, which is a bigger-engined version of the popular Datsun 180B SSS.
>
> Both 260Z and 710 are big on the international rally scene. Both vehicles have won some of the world's toughest rallies - the East Africa Safari enduro.
>
> Howard Marsden, previously Special Vehicles Manager for Ford-Australia, is one of Australia's greatest Competition Managers. He led the Ford Team to many successes on the race track and in rallies from 1971 to 1974, when Ford withdrew from motor sport.
>
> He master-minded victories at Bathurst and in the touring car and manufacturers championships.
>
> Marsden's competition experience goes back to the early 60's when he was contracted by Ford of Europe to oversee their challenges for the Monte Carlo Rally and the Le Mans 24 hours classic.
>
> Datsun sales finished the year 1975 with a 16.78% sales increase over 1974. Retail registration of Datsuns for 1975 reached a record 60,463 vehicles.

Saved and generously donated by Teddy Webber

car that arrived in Australia with ECGI early in '75, and the Aaltonen/Souminen car also from the '75 Cross. We ran all three in various events that year.

Possibly when Howard realised he had a novice mechanic he decided I'd benefit from an experienced mentor, or maybe he knew we'd need more hands to run two vehicles in most events, anyway, he arranged for Bill Evans to join the team. What a terrific bloke to work with – I was so lucky to have had such an experienced mentor and teacher, albeit for just a few months. Minutia I clearly remember involves his showing me how to grind the valve shim caps on the bench grinder when I was trying to adjust the valve clearances on one of the LZ18 engines – a bit agricultural by today's standard but it was all we had and it worked well. I also remember him teaching me how to oxy weld the cracks in the very thin floor of the 240Z from underneath it on the hoist – a continuing job due to already thin metal and the pounding of stones coming off the front wheels.

Sadly, before the Southern Cross that year, Bill decided he needed to return to his own business and departed. Enter Barry Nelson. He'd worked for Alan Moffat and had known Howard from the time they'd both been racing V8s in the U.S.

Our new team's debut event was the open, daylight special-stage, Overture Rally, held at the end of January in the Mt Disappointment Forest, north of Melbourne. George and Monty ran their '75 Cross 710 and won convincingly in a 72-car, Victorian who's who field. A fine first-up result.

Our first serious event though was **The Castrol International.** Fury/Suffern ran as Car #4 and finished second by less than a minute to Greg Carr/Wayne Gregson again in the yellow 180B SSS running as Car #1. It was a furious tussle with both taking turns at the lead and leaving the rest in their wake. But for several punctures Fury could easily have won. It was always hard to beat Greg on his home turf though,

Fury and Suffern crashing through an ACT creek crossing.

especially when he was usually seeded first and therefore most often had the advantage of a dust-free run. Dunkerton and Beaumont placed third in the 240Z as Car #9 (lining up with his Channel 9 sponsorship). There is a stirring recounting of this event on Shannon's website that's well worth a read – Datsun 180B SSS: Nissan's outstanding 1970s rally 'Carr' – (https://www.shannons.com.au/club/news/datsun-180b-sss-nissans-outstanding-1970s-rally-carr)

We'd entered a second 710 as Car #2 for Peter Wherrett/Alan Cummine, making another episode for Peter's TV program, Torque. Despite having a world record size support crew, they finished mid-field somewhere.

The crew included Howard, Bill Evans, John Armitage, John Bosua, Barry Nelson, Richard Power and me. Oh, and the Wherrett entourage and some Nissan execs. There was some tripping over each other going on.

Looking good, so far. Wherrett before the start of the '76 Castrol

It proved to be a reasonably successful result in our first major event under Howard for the newly corporatised Datsun Rally Team, but at times during 1976 there must have been some head scratching at head office, wondering if they shouldn't have given the motorsport budget to Gerry Ball. Ball was given the use of the Aaltonen (then Wherrett) 710 after Greg's Castrol win, and he proceeded to win the Holden Dealers International in the Latrobe Valley and place third to Fury and Dunkerton in the North Eastern ARC round that year.

Tom Snooks, in his excellent *'History of The Australian Rally Championship 1968-1988'* wrote: "The ARC series had not yet developed into the truly national competition it was designed for. Over the years, rising costs, the occasional poorly-run event and what many considered as ridiculous vehicle eligibility regulations all combined to prevent the ARC from becoming a top series. In 1976 certainly the weather played a part with the projected first round, the Mazda House Rally, being twice postponed and then finally cancelled because of heavy rain. Organisational difficulties caused problems, with the West Australian round so poorly organised that competing crews went on strike at one stage rather than continue. The South Australian round had no pre-event publicity and was rewarded with the smallest field for a major event for many years. The Bega Valley Rally wasted the entire first of its two nights by using uncompetitive roads.

Vehicle regulations did not help either. Victorian George Fury, driving a Datsun 710, won three of the four rounds he contested but the vehicle was not eligible for championship points. This happened despite the fact that the 710 was an homologated car eligible to run in the Southern Cross Rally and any other major International events.

In the end Ross Dunkerton/Jeff Beaumont (Datsun 240Z) won the series, well clear of the second placed Dean Rainsford/Graham West (Porsche Carrera RS), and it was Dunkerton's successive drivers' championship. He was the only driver to contest all six rounds. Greg Carr's 180B SSS was subsequently found to be ineligible during the Bega Valley Rally and it dropped out of the series."

So, what would be a fairly disappointing series began in February in WA with The Commonwealth Bank Rally. Rather than tow or ship the LHD works 240Z across to Perth, it made sense for Ross and Jeff to run Ross' own 260Z there. Maybe in sympathy with its LHD brother the 260Z broke a rear suspension arm on the second night while in second place and they could go no further. As stated above the organisation was poor and crews went on strike at one stage after it became evident that some sections had not been checked and were impassable.

In the end Dean Rainsford/Graeme were declared winners in the Porsche Carrera RS with a 30-minute margin over the local 240Z of Danny Bignell/Peter Brainbridge second.

The Marchal Rally based at Ballarat, Victoria attracted a much stronger field. It was characterised by tight, twisty roads with stumps ready to bite corner-cutters. Fury/Suffern set a blistering pace and won the event outright, although unjustly the car was not eligible for ARC points, allowing the Dunkerton/Beaumont LHD 240Z team to take the points as Ross began hitting his straps with the LHD beast. Greg Car/Wayne Gregson should have taken second but their 180B SSS was also deemed ineligible for 1976, allowing Dean Rainsford/Graeme West in the Porsche to inherit second place.

Consternation at service as Ross tells of hitting something hard with the LH Rear. Spectators L to R: Bill's mate, Sunshine Sam, Bill Evans, HRM and the culprit.

The Bega Valley Rally in S.E. NSW that year attracted a good field and, from Tom Snooks' book, "...was, as usual, conducted over two nights in the June long weekend. Run over 950 kilometres, it was a mixture of good and great roads." Conditions were generally so good that many stages were uncompetitive due to the organiser's inability to set fast enough average speeds meaning that several leading crews were able to 'clean-sheet' (better the time set and therefore lose no points). The leading places were, however, closely fought throughout, with Dunkerton/Beaumont in the 'works' LHD 240Z finishing just two points clear of the Rainsford/West Porsche Carrera RS. The Fury/Suffern 710 had led outright until after the last division break, later withdrawing with what was reported as a blown head gasket. As you'll remember, they were in any case, ineligible for championship points.

Fury at speed on the very quick roads around Bega

The Rally Renault, held in the mid-north of SA began and ended at Port Augusta and used the Flinders Ranges, visiting the magnificent Wilpena Pound. Sadly, it was probably the least publicised ARC for many years and as a result attracted a small field. Dunkerton and Rainsford fought it out early until the Porsche was damaged in a wash-away and Dunkerton/Beaumont found themselves with a considerable lead and were able to cruise to the finish, thereby claiming the championship lead.

Compared to the other rounds this year, the North Eastern Car Club produced a near faultless North Eastern Rally. New to the ARC series this year and run in the country between Wangaratta and Bright in Victoria, it was conducted over three divisions totalling 600 kms.

The weather, too, was perfect and the event attracted a top-class field. Fury, Dunkerton and Carr fought hard and placed outright first, second and third respectively, but with the 240Z the only one of the three cars eligible for points, Dunkerton/Beaumont were declared winners and took the points. With Rainsford's demise early in the event ensuring the Datsun team's '76 ARC lead unassailable.

Despite appalling weather, the Warana Rally in southern Queensland was well organised and had been well promoted – definitely worthy of its

ARC status. It was run over two very wet nights and, for the third time that year, George and Monty in their 710 won outright, finishing more than 30 minutes ahead. Ineligible for the ARC however, locals Murray Coote/Brian Marsden in a borrowed Datsun 1600 did well and were declared winners with Dunkerton/Beaumont placing second after a fire (grass caught above the exhaust), bent steering and fuel pump troubles had delayed them.

Feeding time for a thirsty works 240Z at the '76 Warana Rally

Peter Corkran has a memory of a small event run before the Cross in 1976: *"[Nissan] ran three 710's at the front of the 1976 Mountain Rally which started at the Hazelwood Pondage [West Gippsland] as a warmup for the Southern Cross. Two great memories, Maudie and I were car one in the ex Bob Phillips Corolla KE10 and all the Japanese service crews laughed at us!!! Then, we couldn't believe the incredible lines the 710s were taking on the pristine roads, something I had never seen before."*

I was not able to fully support these memories with evidence and I now believe it to be a confluence of two events Peter is remembering. The Mid Eastern Rally was held immediately before the 'Cross and the Holden Dealers International held immediately after. In the former Fury/Suffern ran as Car #00 and Aaltonen/Beaumont ran as Car #0. Three 710s were run in the latter, Mehta/Mortimer placed third in Car #2, Fury/Suffern were second in Car #4 and Carr/Gregson won in Car #6. See below.

Aaltonen & Beaumont running as Car Zero in the '76 Mid Eastern Rally prior to SCR decals etc.

The Southern Cross International Rally

Having entered two 710s in the Southern Cross in 1974 (plus a 180B SSS for George), and three in '75, for 1976 a total of six works 710s were entered. For internationals: Källström/Bonhomme Car #3, Mehta/Mortimer Car #4, Aaltonen/Beaumont Car #7, and Walfridsson/Godden Car #16, and for locals: Fury/Suffern Car #8 and Carr/Gregson Car #10 (a Group 2 car supported in the Cross by Gerry Ball's Canberra-based team.)

Sadly the LHD 240Z and Dunkerton could not be accommodated in our team but, not to be left out, Ross entered his own 260Z as Car #13 with Ben Williams navigating.

All hands on deck. Mehta/Mortimer in service, '76 Cross

As it turned out the event was a major disappointment in a string of Southern Cross disappointments for Datsun, although at the beginning of the last division, for one team at least, it was looking so promising.

Fury started the event suffering with the effects of bronchitis but drove brilliantly to be leading the event at the end of the first, second and third divisions, despite being locked in a tight battle with Cowan.

Aaltonen/Beaumont had retired during the first night while in the lead. They hit a fast and rough creek crossing causing the engine to move forward sufficiently for the fan to puncture the radiator. The engine overheated and blew a head gasket soon after. Jeff says: *"Rauno was quick to point out our speed to Nissan's Japanese bosses who were present, and sign up a place in the team for next year's event."*

Also on the first night, Carr's 710, with a deflating rear tyre, disappeared over a cliff, thankfully without injury to the crew and with little damage to the car but with no chance to recover inside late time. Dunkerton retired the 260Z late on the second night with severely bent steering after getting caught out by a wash-away. Källström retired on the final night with engine failure. Ho hum.

There was some Datsun skulduggery afoot that we Australian crew weren't made fully aware of. At the end of the third night, at our service base at the Total service station in Port Macquarie, we were told that we'd be changing the engine in Fury's car for precautionary reasons. This was contrary to the rules and it became obvious the Japanese were well aware of this as a wall of tyres was quickly erected at the mouth of the service bay behind George's car. From memory the job was done exclusively by Japanese mechanics while we Australians did the scheduled component replacement and servicing of the remaining 710s on the forecourt.

I'm sure I bought their explanation at the time but I do wonder now. It wasn't usual to take a spare engine on a Southern Cross. Obviously the engine number would need to match the logbook at post-event scrutineering, so does that mean a spare engine without a number was brought and the block was stamped before it went into the car? Or maybe a pre-existing number was changed that night? Could it mean that George had been given a non-legal engine for the event and, as he was holding a strong lead in the event at that stage, a compliant engine had to be fitted in order not to be caught out post event? This seems pretty likely now but I doubt we'll ever know.

Anyway, Fury/Suffern had a good lead for 3,150 kms of the 3,300 total until their differential failed while far from service and they were out, allowing the worst of all results for Datsun – another big win for Andrew Cowan's Mitsubishi Lancer. Such is luck in the Southern Cross – if it's not running for you (or maybe if you try to bend the rules) you'll break down somewhere very remote. It was left to Shekhar/Adrian Mortimer to salvage a little respect for us, coming in third and Per Inge Walfridsson/Peter Godden, who'd probably been intended as the hare but had turned into a battered tortoise, finished sixth after a rollover in Div. 1 and a side-swipe to a large tree during Div. 3. Walfridsson's left foot braking style sure was a sight to behold and a great memory to take away though!

George's to lose. Lined up in position order for the start of Day 4

Although privately entered, Iwashita/Yasuoka had an arrangement with Datsun team management to service their LZ16-engined PB210 in the Cross. This was done from a rented Transit van driven by Chris Brown who was chauffeuring Mr Gun and, I think, Mr Sasamoto.

The Holden Dealers International in Southern Gippsland, Victoria, was the next event for us, straight after returning from the 'Cross.

Just to show you can't always rely on things you read on a rally car. Fred Gocentas making an early appearance with Greg Carr!

Greg Car with Fred Gocentas ran as Car #6, again in the 710 they'd begun the 'Cross in. George and Monty used the Kalstrom/Bonhomme SCR car (presumably with another engine), and Mehta/Mortimer used the Fury/Suffern SCR car (presumably with another diff). They finished first, second and third consecutively.

One month later Carr/Gregson, again in their 'Cross car, won The Kleber Alpine in north eastern Victoria. Noteably for this event, the car carried the MA7359 carnet plates, indicating a lazy bonnet swap following the damage done in their SCR mishap.

Shekhar Metha laying down some of those tyre marks that Peter Corkran remembered from the '76 HDI

With Gerry Ball's team supporting Greg, I was free to enter my own 1600 so Mark Holmes (driving) and I started as Car #34 and managed sixth outright and first in Group 4 (driver's rating).

As a bonus, after the Southern Cross and instead of the Alpine in 1976, Ross' 260Z was flown to New Caledonia for the NC Safari, a round of the South Pacific Championship. As a service crew, part timer

Nick Watt and myself flew with Ross, wife Rosann, and navigator Brian McGuirk across to Noumea and stayed at the luxurious Chateau Royale Hotel (later to become Club Med Noumea) to relax up for the gruelling, three-division event.

The rally had several top competitors entered including New Zealander, Mike Marshall in an RS1800 Escort, Achim Warmbold, BMW 320, local champion and past winner, Jean Ragnotti and Shekhar Mehta in a pair of Datsun 710s and Doug Stewart/ John Dawson-Damer, Mitsubishi Lancer, to name but a few reputable crews.

A short break in the 1976 New Caledonia Safari

Sadly though the event became a farce when, on the second division, the generally poor instructions became so bad that the entire field became hopelessly lost in a maze of nickel mining roads and with everyone eventually out of late running time the event was abandoned.

After a night's sleep it was decided to run Div 3 as a separate event so the twenty-five crews able to ready their cars, headed off anew.

When they returned to Noumea late that night and scores were tallied, Jean Ragnotti was declared the winner and crews retired to their beds. A simple error was discovered while they slept however and, when correctly totalled, Mehta was found to have won. As there'd been no protest within the allowable time however, the correction could not be made. What a shambles!

Although winning some stages, Ross had been forced to retire during the afternoon with electrical problems. I think we made it back to the Chateau in time for happy hour though, so all was well.

At the end of 1976, as we began the move from South Melbourne to our new and much larger workshop at Braeside, **Jamie Drummond**, who'd been helping part time in the later part of the year, joined us full time and quickly became a valued part of the team. The new location was on Lower Dandenong Rd, Braeside, beside Nissan Australia's Parts Warehouse and Distribution Centre and had, prior to the opening of the new Head Office in South Dandenong, been used as the new vehicle Pre-

Delivery Centre. It consisted of about one third of a high, all-steel shed near the corner of Lower Dandenong and Boundary Roads. It had a small office at the Eastern end and a high roller door on the southern side, exiting onto a wide concrete apron for the building's full length and then a

Nissan's parts facility at Braeside, Vic C.1971. The LH end of the large shed in the foreground was our rally workshop from 1976 to 1981

huge gravel-paved vehicle holding yard which, when we first arrived was half full of cars and light commercials but gradually emptied, leaving an excellent place to "do circle work" in old rally cars, according to Jamie ;-)

We bought a second 2-post hoist and were able to spread out, beginning to create separate spaces for engine, gearbox/diff, suspension/brakes, servicing etc.

Jamie remembers: "I did my first Southern Cross in one of the blue 4-cyl E20 vans... f—ing scary with all that weight, cross-ply tyres and no brakes. I drove that one to Sydney with Johnny Bosua (he had the worst smelling feet ever! A very good teacher though :-) but Howard then put me in another van with one of the Japanese mechanics [Heichan Cato]. I don't think JB liked my driving either, ha ha ha."

Heichan still looking pretty cool while Jamie re-stows the gear after a good Southern Cross fanging in the blue E20

With the LHD 240Z looking rather the worse for wear – several cracks had developed around suspension mounts – after the Lutwyche

Rally in 1976, Ross had it shipped over to West Australia and, after giving it some thought, decided to strip the good stuff from it and put them in his 260Z. It's a terrible shame that the old works shell was apparently left somewhere to rust away. Imagine what it would be worth today!

Ross' 260Z sporting at least the works 240Z light bar. Still in good shape at the beginning of day 2 at Port Macquarie in the 1976 Southern Cross Rally…

And just to show that George isn't always serious….

Who else can we see here enjoying the presentation for the 1976 Holden Dealers International?

Johnny Bosua, never happier than when underneath a Datsun rally car. Here George's 710 at the 1976 Holden Dealers International.

1977

Until 1977 we'd run the cars from Japan pretty much as they'd arrived here, modifications being restricted to crew accommodation and facilities. By this time though, we were beginning to seriously Australianise the 710s – softer springs, lower ground clearance, tweaking some suspension angles, engine modifications, lighter cars and Australian paint livery, etc. After many years in the doldrums, the Australian Championship series was hotting up with more serious, better financed, quicker competition and finally, sensible eligibility regulations.

Also early in '77 we were 'put on the clock'. The large spare parts installation next door to our workshop had many employees and a clock card system was in place whereby workers were required to punch their timecard when beginning and ending a 'shift' – these cards were then used to calculate wages. Someone (I assume Lionel Sparrow, the head-office-based boss of Spare Parts) decided we DRT members should also comply. This decision rather backfired on management as we used to do several all-nighters and then, when we'd go off on rallies we were told not to clock off until we returned – often not until Monday or sometimes later. The 'program' that worked out wages auto switched to time and a half and then double time after so many hours so we racked up a lot of paid time which led to a lot of pay. For three years or so we were making in the vicinity of $30K, which was not too shabby back then. I think it was in 1980 that HM announced on one of his visits that we were to be taken off the timecards and given a salary based on our last FY's pay – the timecard system had no doubt seen an escalation of pay and they wanted to lock in a set salary – not sure, but it was their idea and we were only too happy to comply.

There were behind the scenes rumblings at Braeside of which I had no memory but was reminded of by Jamie:

> *"Do you remember we were being blamed for petrol going missing?* [There was a petrol bowser at the spare parts premises which we had access to on an honesty system which required keeping records including rego numbers and signing for petrol taken] *You and I were working one Sunday afternoon and our cars were out of sight and we sprung Lionel Sparrow taking petrol without filling in the book! You told John (boss of Spares). They setup a security photographer out on the boundary and took photos of him and his*

mates filling their cars the next weekend and no record in the book. Busted! He was probably going to set us up but they found out and he was given the flick!"

Before the first ARC round, George and Monty ran The Overture Rally, an open event in Victoria, as a shake down and try out of the work we'd been doing. I've not been able to ascertain the results of the event but hopefully we learnt something.

In Tom Snooks' book, he says: *"After a number of years of the ARC languishing in the doldrums as a second-rate series, things really came to life in 1977."*

And, *"Rally enthusiasts could hardly have dared hope for a better opening to the series than the North Eastern Rally."* Tom's event-by-event account of all the ARC events in '77 make for exciting reading and I heartily encourage you to get a copy of his book if this sort of writing floats your boat. I'll be content here to recount the placings and the failures.

So, first serious event for '77 was The North Eastern Rally in NE Victoria. It was a hard fought affair and standings after the first division: Morrow (in the now much faster HDT Gemini) followed by Dunkerton (in his rejuvenated 260Z), Portman (in the Les Collins built Datsun 1600) showing promise of what was to come, Watson (in the Gerry Ball prepared 120Y), and Fury, in his '75 Cross 710.

Fury's 710 at full squat under power. The A-arms didn't cope.

In Div. 2 Dunkerton and Fury chased down Morrow but then the 710's rear suspension broke and Dunko lost time in a transport section so that at the end it was the Morrow/Shepheard Gemini first – a rare ARC finish, let alone win – one minute ahead of Dunkerton/Beaumont, and Geoff Portman/Ross Runnalls a further three minutes back in the 1600.

In March, for **The Castrol International** in Canberra, George and Monty used Harry Källström's '76 Cross 710 to run as Car #2. Greg Carr had only recently started with the Ford team and he dominated the event to give them good promise for the future. George and Monty placed second.

A hungry looking 710 ready to do the business.

The Rally of the West was again run South of Perth in still and dusty conditions but this year had attracted a much larger entry and was conducted at a much improved standard. Fury/Suffern began well and led at the division break with locals Bignell/Bousfield in a 240Z second, Dunkerton/Beaumont in Ross' 260Z, third and Morrow/Shepheard fourth in the now quick Holden Gemini. Early in the night division, both Fury and Morrow had offs, losing them time, Dunkerton punctured. The event continued in such vane with the leading positions changing due to dust, off-road excursions and punctures until, at the end, Dunkerton had won, Fury had come second by twelve minutes and Clive Slater, in a Corolla Sprinter, had come third, a further six minutes back.

Earlier in the year it had been decided (somehow) to run a G60 Patrol in the **Hattah BP Desert Rally** in NW Victoria – the New Commercial Sales Dept. trying to get in on the act I guess. Barry Nelson set to on the straight-off-the-showroom-floor Patrol and had more than halved its weight before lunch. No rally car wants a 4-litre, 6-cyl, cast iron push rod engine, or a gigantic 3-speed gearbox and transfer case, and it

Wild Bill doing one of his stints in the hot-rodded Patrol

probably wouldn't need a huge front diff, so all that stuff was discarded. A SOHC (FIA) engine and Option 1 gearbox from a 710 was slipped in, big Bilsteins fitted all round, competition seats and 4-point seat belts bolted in and it was nearly ready to go.

The Hattah was a rugged event and usually the driving was alternatingly shared over its four loops, so who better to teach Peter Wherrett some relevant driving skills than (Wild) Bill Evans? The event was filmed by Wherrett's team and an episode of Torque (a weekly motoring TV program of the times) was made from it. They ended up doing quite well in the event (31st out of the 200, 4-wheeled vehicles) but would have done much better had Wherrett not rolled the beast and Bill had been able to drive all four loops. Michael Baker won the event outright in a purpose-built off-road buggy. I don't know if the Patrol ever did another event or indeed what was its fate.

The Torque episode made of the event is definitely worth a watch, if only to experience the surreal sight and sound of a G60 Patrol with a 710 engine and to see Wild Bill in action close up. Plus of course to see Barry Nelson at his sartorial best including the flash tartan hat, kicking out the windscreen after the rollover, and to see a very young Jamie Drummond on refuelling duty.

The Lutwyche Village Rally in Queensland was usually run in September but, so as not to collide with the London to Sydney Marathon event that year, it was rescheduled to May. There had been rain in previous days so most competitors were relieved to not be battling dust for a change.

Lined up in Brisbane for the start of much carnage.

Big spectator crowds came out as well as most contenders for the ARC but very soon after the start competitors began dropping like flies – mostly mechanical problems but also some driver-inflicted damage. Firstly Morrow's Gemini with unknown gremlins within metres of the start of the very first stage, then Dunkerton's 260Z lost its sump plug followed quickly by its oil and then its forward motion. At the first break, Carr's Escort led Watson's 120Y and Fury's 710 by just one minute, with

Stewart's Lancer a further minute back.

The carnage continued and in the early hours of the following morning Fury retired with a broken distributor drive followed shortly by the Holden Gemini with a failed water pump. All top contenders DNF'd so that a very sorry looking scoreboard greeted us back at base. Doug Stewart/Neil Faulkner had won in a Lancer and Bob Riley/Brian Hope in a Galant second. A local Datsun 1600 had come third. A long trip for most for very little.

The Bega Valley Rally on the South coast of NSW in June was our first event in the new Australian colour scheme with only 'Datsun' signage. After the rather busy livery we'd first run at the '75 Cross, the cars looked clean and had lost much of their 'big hips' look. This was also Dunko's first event in a Datsun 710, having been brought back into the full works fold.

Fury/Suffern, at '77 Bega. First event in Australian war paint

Watson, Fury and Carr were fast out of the blocks but this was again a very slippery event and it wasn't long before cars were sliding off – often into trees. Morrow/Shepheard in the Holden Dealer Team Gemini was first, then Bonhomme's 1600, then Fury, who was able to recover and continue – interesting to note that the best drivers tend only to hit trees gently. Carr had problems when a rear wheel came loose at high speed then Fury had another off and Dunkerton, still coming to grips with his 710, was also off and impaled his radiator with a tree branch.

Dunko was an early retirement on Day 2 when his engine let go. Fury lost more time with fuel pump trouble and everyone it seemed was having a bad event, either off the road or with mechanical trouble. In the end Carr/Gocentas in the Escort RS2000 had done best to win on 40 points down, with Fury/Suffern second on 45. Daryl (Revs) Rowney/ Robbie Wilson in their Datsun 1600 were next best, down 53.

So, with four different winners from four rounds, the stage was set for an exciting finale with any of the top five drivers able to win the championship in the last round.

There was then quite a long gap (mid June 'til mid September) during which we were able to do some further development work.

It paid off too, as the final round for the year, **The Endrust Rally** in SA provided us a fine quinella with Fury/Suffern winning, down 34 points, and Dunko/Beauy second on 40. The Morrow/Shepheard team Gemini must have been relieved to finally get on the rostrum, down 42. There was little to separate Bond and Carr who placed fourth and fifth, down 46 and 47 respectively.

A happy crew at the end of the Endrust Forest Rally near Adelaide

The organisers had apparently been inspired by the success of the Castrol International and came up with a similar event of three divisions with 420 kms competitive. First and third divisions were held in daylight and featured quarter-minute timing. The event attracted the best field of the year and was well promoted too, so that, even with live coverage, a real novelty at that time, huge crowds turned up to spectate in the Mount Crawford Forest causing traffic jams on roads from Adelaide.

At first division end Fury led narrowly from Carr, Morrow, Shinozuka (Lancer), Riley (Galant), Dunkerton and Bond, all snapping at his heels.

The second (night) division, though uncompetitive due to many 'cleanable' stages, had serious repercussions due to dust and missed vital instructions – Carr in particular losing time and any chance of winning the event or the ARC title. Fury started Div. 3 with a handy lead, with Dunkerton closest then Morrow in the Gemini third.

And that was how it finished, with a fifth different winner for the series and the result providing, for the first time, an unbreakable tie for the Championship between Fury/Suffern and Dunkerton/Beaumont. A very good ARC year for the Datsun Rally Team.

George Fury had what seemed an inspired thought. Rather than the

A-arm independent rear suspension, common to several Datsun models of the time, including the 710, and which caused quite radical changes to rear wheel toe-in and camber as the wheels travelled up and down, a beam axle running behind the diff and linked forward to the body (known as deDion rear suspension) would keep the wheels vertical and aligned. This had to be a step in the right direction he figured. With Howard's approval, Barry Nelson was left to the task of fabricating the required components in the workshop while the rest of us, together with the Japanese contingent, prepared for, then set off on the Cross.

Baz, gas axe always handy, working away at building a de Dion rear end for a 710!

Pete Davis contributed several memories to my efforts to write this book. The first of them can go here:

Pete Davis catches a few Zs while Shinoda san has another fag

"*Memory is not all that good* [better than mine I have to concede!] *but Rauno and Jeff had won the '77 Cross in the 710. That was my first outing, driving Mr. Shinoda* [Japanese team manager of the time] *around after Bill Evans couldn't make it. After joining the team full-time* [early 1978] *we built the 'lightweight 710's' for the '78 Australian season.*"

The Southern Cross International Rally

For the first time a round of the FIA World Drivers Cup, the SCR this year was less of a trial and more like a long special stage event. Many of the 'horror' roads from previous events were avoided, reducing the total distance by some 600 kms plus the transport section times were eased. The results were obviously intended to be decided by competitive section times. Electronic timing equipment was flown in and stages timed to hundredths of minutes, penalties applied to the second and based on competitors' times over the time allowed.

The withdrawal of the Mitsubishi works team was a blow for the event and it meant the absence of six time winner Andrew Cowan, which made the Datsun clean sweep of the first three places seem a little hollow. (We soon got over it.) The presence of the works Ford team though, ensured there was no lack of quality opposition with Colin Bond/John Dawson-Damer in an RS2000 Escort and Greg Carr/Fred Gocentas, for the first time in an RS1800 Cosworth BDG-powered Escort. The Holden Dealer Team was also there, now with Wayne Bell/George Shepheard in the Gemini.

Four apparently new 710s had arrived for the '77 Cross to join two that were already in the country from past events. New cars were numbered #1 for Makinen/Liddon, #3 for Aaltonen/Beaumont, #4 for Källström/Billstam, and #6 for Fury/Suffern. The two recycled cars were prepared, entered and serviced by Gerry Ball Tuning and were #7 for Dunkerton/Pigram, and #12 for Watson/Godden. There was also a PB210 with 1600cc LZ DOHC engine for Mehta/Mortimer as Car #5.

Makinen showed his class, winning six of the first 10 stages and being second fastest on two others. At the end of Div. 1 he led Carr's Escort by more than two minutes. Next were Källström, Aaltonen, Fury in 710s, all covered by one minute, then Bond in the second Escort, Watson and Dunkerton in 710s and Mehta in the PB210 spread over nearly ten minutes.

Carr's Escort foreground with Mehta's 210 then the four new 710s of Fury, Källström, Aaltonen and Makinen

In Div. 2, Carr whittled away Makinen's lead and by the end of the fifth stage had overtaken him, there to stay till the last night. At Div. 2 end though, Carr led Makinen to Aaltonen, Källström, Bond, Fury, Watson, Shinozuka, Mehta and Dunkerton, around 28 minutes covering those ten positions.

Carr, now with the dust-free run, but driving brilliantly, extended his lead in Div. 3 . Dunkerton/Pigram retired with sheared rear wheel studs allowing Bell/Shepheard into the top ten by the division three's end.

Div. 4 included the marathon 236km stage between Bellingen and Kempsey. Could any of the Datsuns better the Escort on the last night? It didn't begin well as Makinen hit a rock and split his engine's sump forcing his retirement.

Most of the top competitors still running had arranged the setup of a servicing point on a side road somewhere near the middle of the long section to refuel and change tyres in their own time. Carr's alternator failed before this stage and with no replacement available (special Boreham works part) he had no choice but to enter the long stage on battery power – two of them, one for a single driving light and one for the ignition!

We were among the first service crews to arrive at the side road. It was no highway but we were able to park in the scrub leaving the dirt track just clear. To our consternation the official on duty allowed other arriving service vehicles to park on the other side of the track so that there seemed quite a narrow path between them all.

To our delight, the first car to appear was a 710! And what an experience – god but the cars sound good going hard out in the forest. It was a still night way out in the bush on a very fast road. The drivers are fighting over seconds and thoroughly in the groove. Rauno approached the intersection at full noise, lights blazing, braked late, flicked, hit the apex, braked and pulled up accurately alongside our van, 40 metres up the road. We had two new wheels on and 80 litres of fuel in before we actually knew what was happening and he was well off again before we could hear Harry coming. Harry's stop was a repeat performance – refuel, new tyres, off up the road to find room for a three (or so) point turn, scream back past us and throw it back onto the route.

But next came Fury. Where Rauno and Harry had stopped alongside the van then performed a three point turn in order to get back to the rally route, George braked and then handbrake turned a neat 180° between the two rows of service vehicles. Everyone's jaws hit the road except our crew who had quick work to perform before we could watch them go –

and then we just stood back and laughed. We'd have sworn there wasn't a car's length between the rows of service vehicles but no paintwork was touched. We left there on a high.

Later we heard that Greg and Fred arrived at that optional service point by torchlight, by then well out of the placings. We also heard though, that George and Monty had had a huge crash near the end of the section and were out of the event.

So, Aaltonen, Källström, Watson – first, second, third to Datsun 710s. Finally a win (for Jeff Beaumont on his ninth attempt) and clearly our best result at a Southern Cross International Rally. Slightly soured as it was though by George and Monty's demise, battling an unfavourably handling car for a gruelling 4-day event and within sight of the finish, they'd have come third if only…

Four or five of us went in with a van and trailer to recover Car #6. It was upside down in a ditch with its off-side rear wheel missing, broken through the stub axle, and every panel battered. We walked back up the road and George showed us where the accident began, it was a long way – he was just about to grab fifth, just over a rise…

Victory at last. Rauno and Jeff cw champers

So close and yet so far. Fury and Suffern, f'd and far from home

This was our last event for 1977. We did not run a car in the '77 Repco Alpine so this left me free to run with Ian Swan in his 120Y – we came fifth after Carr and Bond in the works Escorts, Chris Power's 1600, and Gil Davis' 1600. Second in our class ☺

Aaltonen's winning car was shipped back to Japan and still has a place of pride at the Zama Museum. Fury's wrecked car was stripped back in Melbourne and eventually crushed at Sims Metal, and Watson's 710 was shipped to New Caledonia for Dunko and Beauy to use and win the Safari there late that year. Dunkerton's car disappeared into the Canberra black hole.

Place mat from the 1977 Southern Cross Rally presentation dinner

So ended Total Oil's Southern Cross International Rally sponsorship

On our return to Melbourne there was a de Dion rear end to test in one of the cars (not sure now which one was used) but it proved to be no better, time-wise, up and back on our Mt Slide testing road. Despite the big angle changes with the IRS, it did work pretty damned well so, with the Stanzas not far off (not that the workers knew that at the time), the de Dion project went no further.

1978

FIA Group 5 was adopted as the eligibility for the ARC and the Southern Cross International Rally for 1978. (The Group 5 regulations were further relaxed as Australian Group G – the 'almost anything goes' class.)

Some time shortly after the first Stanza arrived in Australia in '78, I began working on adapting an LZ twin cam head to the LR20B SOHC motor that came with the new Stanza. The plan was to build a larger capacity and more powerful twin cam engine. See the story about the LZ development in the chapter about the engines on page 187

Our first event for 1978 however, was again a shake-down but this time on the other side of the country. We had the two 710s and two 6-cyl E20s trucked over to Perth in time for WA's first State Championship round in which John Large navigated for George (see Monty's account of his relationship with George in the section on Team Members). Other than George deciding he'd rather stick with Monty, I think it went pretty well and we all flew home leaving everything behind, except the Rosco/Beauy intercom, which had been playing up.

Ten days later we flew back to Perth for ARC round one for the year,

The Rally of the West.

For 1978 we had another revision to the war paint, which really only amounted to a wider red stripe along the side. However, after the two cars had been resprayed from their international Southern Cross livery, to the predominantly blue and white scheme, we'd run out of time to add the red strip and the sign writing before the cars had to leave on the truck. In just the blue and white, I actually thought they looked very sharp. We were able to add 'Total' (new sponsor for '78 ARC) and 'Datsun' stickers after we unloaded them in Perth. We were also running with four 7" headlamps (or six, where

My favourite 710 pic. See the funnnel under Beauy's chin?

allowed) set into the grill rather than the previous year's, two plus external driving lamps. I thought the look of the 710s reached its peak that year.

So, looking good, but we'd managed to leave the repaired intercom back in Melbourne! Nothing phases a Ross Dunkerton on a mission – he had someone dash off to the local shops and come back with a funnel and a roll of plastic tubing. Yep, one end nylon-tied up inside his helmet, the other stuck onto the funnel and that tied to Beauy's helmet. I was so amused to have that memory come back to life when I found the photo (previous page) where you can clearly see the funnel. It obviously did them no harm as they won the event and this was no doubt where the hilarious yarn about Beauy sucking Dunko's ear drum out began.

The Datsun/Ford/Holden three-year battle was now in full-swing and many stages were hard fought with often just a second or two covering the first four or five cars.

So, in this event, Greg Carr in the RS1800 Escort speared off early and injured his thumb, costing them 17 minutes (he was later to have his forearm put in plaster and they were forced to retire.) Dave Morrow, standing in for Colin Bond, was in the second (RS2000) Escort but he and John Dawson-Damer didn't feature in the results. The engine of the Bell/Shepheard Holden Gemini blew close to the end of the night division. The pointy end of the battle was dominated by Fury and Dunkerton and the lead changed several times.

In the end Dunkerton/Beaumont won, down 74, to Fury/Suffern on 81, then Bell/Shepheard on 107.

The Castrol International Rally

Rossco enjoying his special stage Datsun ute

Probably because Nissan had turned their motorsport focus toward the Stanza and was no longer interested in marketing via the 710, it was decided a more novel entry might be in order for the '78 Castrol. Possibly inspired by the Holden Ute that was always run in the Castrol by a local crew, maybe this was an opportunity to give Nissan commercial vehicles another plug. It was decided (probably over a few Chardonnays) to build a rally car out of a 620 Utility!

John Bosua got the job and a new J15 (1500cc push-rod) engined, white 620 was delivered to BGM Motors in Vermont and JB set to work on it. Similar to the Patrol from the previous year, it was engine and gearbox out, single cam FIA-headed LR18 with Option 1 gearbox and custom tail shaft in, rally front hubs fitted and Sumitomo calipers adapted. This time there were also vented discs and 4-spots for the rear. Bilsteins all round, rally seats and lights and some war paint and it was just about ready to go. Now, who do we get to drive a non-serious, almost comical rally 'car', in an International Special-Stage event on national TV?

To give the new weapon a bit of shake-down, The Magic Carpet Rally (an open special stage event) beginning at the timber yard at Narbethong just east of the Black Spur in the Dandenong Ranges, was chosen and I was given the navigating job! We were Car #1. From memory there was a 50 metre transport section before the first stage through the yard – in and out and around the stacks of lumber with tiny intermediate distances between instructions. I'd soon fallen off the route chart and was panicking but did that daunt my clowning-one-minute, laser-focussed-the-next, driver? Not a bit. Dunko has an uncanny ability to see wheel tracks and somehow faultlessly followed Car #0 through at speed. I don't remember much more about the event or the results but I do remember the ute went pretty well and we had a lot of fun. I must have given the beast an elephant stamp and we returned to BGM Motors for a clean and a tweak or two in preparation for the Castrol a fortnight later.

Car #1 in the '78 Castrol was The Stig in a works Saab! For a wet and slippery event he'd be fast and hard to beat. Car #2 was Greg Carr in the works Escort RS1800 and wanting to win the event for a fourth consecutive time but still suffering with a painful wrist. Colin Bond in the RS2000 Escort was Car #4 and following him was the Ute as Car #5, Dunkerton/Mortimer flying a confederate army flag (or maybe it was a scarf) from the radio aerial and looking a bit skittish on the slippery tracks.

Dunko was there with the leading few for the first daylight division but had a rear shocker mount break in the night, costing them several minutes. Servicing on the event were Howard

HM with dirty hands! Giving the crowd a chuckle

(chuckle), Johnny Bosua and Peter Davis (the last two slithering around in the mud on their backs). Wasn't I lucky to have had 'more important' things to do back at the workshop? Both Carr and Blomquist had some trouble in the night but come morning Carr was leading with Stig Blomquist breathing hard down his neck, Bell in the Gemini a way back in third and Dunkerton running mid field but still having a big go. Not to pour (even more) cold water on an intriguing and exciting event, but that was how it finished – Carr/Gocentas with just seconds to Blomquist/West then minutes to Bell/Shepheard and Portman/Runnalls in the 1600 'Grunter' not far back in fourth.

The Lutwyche Village Rally held in coastal forests north of Brisbane was round two of the Australian Championship in '78. The event was innovative in that all competitive sections were timed and scored to the second – not just the daylight-run stages – and also that there was a 'prologue' stage to determine starting order. Adding further pressure for his inclusion in our team, Geoff Portman in his 1600 was fastest on the prelude from Greg Carr, then Queensland Champion Ray Vandersee in his Torana XU1.

Carr and Bond dominated the early stages though and Portman had an early off and was out. Carr led at the Nambour meal break from Dunkerton, Bond, then Fury.

First stage in Div. 2 was 134km and Carr flew, beating Dunko by nearly three minutes. Fury had brake problems plus a failed rear shock absorber, allowing Bond through.

710 in Queensland. Ross with the '78 war paint

These positions held through Div. 3, with Carr protecting his lead while the others tried hard to improve their positions but this was how they finished.

Pete Davis remembers: "...*in the Lutwyche we had perspex windows fitted in the 710s and one blew out. I was a bit worried it might have presented a bit of a problem for the next car which was George Shepheard* with Wayne Bell. I asked George if it was on the road and he replied "no mate we had to drive off the road to get it" !!! [Funny man George Shepheard – very quick on the retort.]

Both Nissan and Ford entered full strength teams again for round three, The Donleee 500 Rally, held in far west New South Wales around the town of Broken Hill on the weekend of 13-14 May. The roads through this desert area were generally fast but rough, the attrition rate reasonably high, no doubt due to the sprint-pace that the tight competition forced on the top teams.

Many heroes and friends here waiting for a start at Broken Hill. Shoot me an email if you think you can add to my list of known names.

One novel feature of the event was two flying laps of the Broken Hill Speedway to begin the competition and some smug looking locals offered $100 for the fastest lap and an extra $100 to anyone who could break the existing lap record. Every national crew broke that lap record, Greg Carr by 2.4 seconds! The locals were somewhat slack-jawed and were no doubt left wondering about their formula for a successful speedway car.

Carr was first to retire with a collapsing front end and this left Dunkerton and Fury to do battle until, while leading, Dunko's engine stopped after having been smoking heavily. It still wasn't popularly accepted that this was bad for one's health.

Division 2 was the main part of the event, beginning at 8.30 pm and running through till almost 9am next morning. George and Monty began amassing a large lead which they almost gave away in the dying stages when they took a wrong road, leading to them doing an extra 21 kms. They lost 16 minutes, cutting their lead to just two. George then took four minutes off second placed Slater/Halloran in the final stage to reassert his dominance. The final margins were Fury, 101 minutes lost to Slater's 107 and Bond's 111.

The event ended mid morning at the old gold mining town of Silverton and in particular, the Silverton Pub, where there was much merriment made and even a Ford vs. Datsun camel race in the main street, to much over-tired hilarity.

In the interests of camaraderie between competitors, service vehicles were switched for the trip back to Broken Hill and there may have been some competition involved. I seem to remember the Ford guys were pretty impressed with our E20s.

Sometime around the time of the Castrol International the first works Stanza arrived. We immediately took it to Mt Slide (North East of Melbourne) to find out what we had. Too much time must have passed since George last drove his Cortina as the live rear axle caught him out and the Stanza went over the side – with Howard in the LH seat! George, Pete Davis, and myself had to work very hard on a Tirfor to get it back up onto the road. No serious damage was done and we had it ready for the Bega rally a couple of weeks later.

First run up Mt Slide – with HM on board. Then oops...

George, myself and Pete D winch it back up to the road.

Pete Davis modestly reminded me further that... *"testing was conducted in a local event, The Goldfields Rally run by the Renault Car Club. Already rear brake issues were becoming apparent as the longevity of the rear brakes was minimal, as was their performance."*

Richard Power drove in that event too. He comments: *"... that was my last special stage rally drive, finishing second to Peter Davis ahead of somebody called Fury in a Stanza, third."*

The Bega Valley Rally in SE NSW was usually run on the Queen's Birthday long weekend in June but heavy rain and severe flooding forced its postponement this year until August. I managed to get the new big twin cam engine finished and installed and we also managed to get the car painted up in our new '78 war paint. We proudly arrived at Bega with one new Stanza for George and Monty and one well-sorted 710SSS for Dunko and Beauy.

Fury/Suffern first serious outing in the new Stanza

The event was in the fashionable format of three divisions: daylight - night - daylight and at the end of the first it was Carr, Fury, Dunkerton equal on 8 points. In the night the lead fluctuated between Carr and Dunkerton, each having a couple of punctures allowing the other through. Behind them was a battle royal involving Bond, Fury and Portman in his very fast 1600. At end Div. 2 it was Carr, three mins ahead of Dunkerton, ahead of Portman – the new Stanza had broken its differential and was out – and that was how the event finished with Carr down 30, Dunkerton (having surrendered) down 43, Bond on 55 and Portman 60. Murray Coote/Brian Marsden in the 120Y a fine sixth with 61, right behind Portman.

Dunko and Beauy lighting up the Bega night

Pete D's memories: *"The car was entered in the 1978 Bega Valley Rally, a round of the Australian Championship where it became apparent that both the differential and rear brakes were issues that required attention if the car was to be reliable. Various rear brake shoe materials were tried including the much-heralded metallic linings, all to no avail though and several shoe changes were required throughout the event.*

The Stanza had to retire with a broken crown wheel and pinion which triggered the decision to redesign the rear driveline and brakes." [See section on development of the Stanza, on page 172]

Shortly after the Bega Rally in '78, three new Stanzas arrived for the Southern Cross – Group 5 twin cams for Aaltonen and Källström and a Group 2 single cam for Dunkerton. Rauno arrived before we went to Adelaide for the Endrust so we grabbed the opportunity to provide a Stanza familiarisation run for him at Mt. Slide plus an entry in the Endrust.

At Mt Slide. Rauno's first time in his new SCR Stanza – Monty standing in as navigator

Another memory snippet from Pete: *"After Barry Nelson [was dismissed] in early '78, Pete Pender filled in for one or two events. I particularly remember him at Bega and then Pete Ryan came on board. A million stories and some fond memories."*

The Endrust Rally, (five weeks later) was again held in forests near Adelaide, SA, and again extensively televised and followed by huge crowds. We'd entered three cars: a 710SSS for Dunkerton/Beaumont, Stanzas for Fury/Suffern and Aaltonen/Mortimer. It did not go well for any of us. Aaltonen retired in the first transport section due to failed timing gear train, Dunk's 710 was fed water instead of fuel at a service point and stopped shortly afterward, and Fury was one of many to get heavily bogged and finished mid field. Colin Bond and John Dawson-Damer won the event, their first in their Australian built copy of Carr's RS1800, and they were followed home by Portman/Runnalls Datsun 1600, Harrowfield/Bonhomme Datsun 1600, Jones/Pearson Mitsubishi Lancer, then two more Datsun 1600s, driven by Pittaway and Rex Muldoon.

Peter Davis has far and away the best memory of the events of 1978 so I'm happy to use the words he's provided me here. The story of the water in the fuel 'churn' goes like this:

"...the water in the fuel episode was at the Endrust and I do know about it and why and how it happened. Jamie had just finished putting a 2.8 engine into our van and we took it to testing at Mt. Slide. On the way home something happened to the cooling system in the van and we needed water. We didn't have a water churn on board only empty fuel churns. We stopped at a creek along the road

at about 1.00am in the morning to fill a churn with water to get the van going. We didn't use all the water and stupidly I didn't empty the water out of the fuel churn, probably thinking we may need some more. The real problem came from the fact that we used to have a lot of partially fuelled churns lying about the place and when it came time to fuel up prior to leaving for the Endrust I just filled all the churns including the one that was still partially filled with water. Totally my fault. Very depressing for me at the time. I think it cost Ross the championship that year."

The Southern Cross International Rally

For the 40th anniversary of the 1978 Southern Cross Rally, my friend Jeff Cameron, wrote a 2-part article on the team's success that year for the Datsun Sports Owners Club magazine. Jeff has recently completed a full restoration of the last of the works Stanzas to arrive in Australia so he has a vital interest in the subject of the article. With his blessing I quote the opening paragraph here.

"*From 1972, the mighty Nissan Motor Company, Japan, threw everything it had into trying to win the prestigious Southern Cross Rally. To the Japanese this event in Australia was held in similar esteem as the gruelling East African Safari in Kenya. Over the years Nissan dispatched its finest works cars from Oppama; bellowing 240Z, prosaic 180B and exotic 710SSS, crewed by world-class drivers like Rauno Aaltonen, Timo Makinen, Harry Källström, Per-Inge Walfridsson and Tony Fall. Supporting the machines were white-gloved factory mechanics directed by Japanese management along with container-loads of tyres and spares. The effort was immense, but it wasn't until 1977 when Rauno Aaltonen and Australian navigator Jeff Beaumont brought a 710SSS home in first place, that the silverware found a place in the Tokyo trophy cabinet. Victory at last. The following year Nissan Japan sent three of its new frontline Datsun Stanza rally cars to take on the world's best in Australia. Could they repeat the win and claim the glory of success for the emerging model?*"

Total Oil largely withdrew its sponsorship for 1978 and the opening was taken up by Travelodge. This from Tom Snooks' History of the Southern Cross Rally: "*...Datsun once again dominated the*

THE DATSUN RALLY TEAM IN AUSTRALIA

Car 1. Rauno Aaltonen & Jeff Beaumont

Car 2. Harry Källström & Claes Billstam

Car 5. Ross Dunkerton & Adrian Mortimer

Car 6. George Fury & Monty Suffern in the car we made ours, and set to pounce on them all.

A tale of 4 Stanzas. Here at SS1 at Amaroo Park entry list with four new model 2-litre 160J Stanzas. Three were prepared in Japan, two being twin cam 16 valve 215 bhp cars for Rauno Altonen and Harry Källström, plus Ross Dunkerton's single cam car with 190bhp, and all three cars had drum brakes in the rear. These cars were serviced mainly by Japanese service crews. The fourth car was locally prepared for George Fury, and had a DOHC 2.2-litre with 222 bhp, a different suspension to the other three and disc brakes on the rear. Australian and Japanese service crews looked after this car under Howard Marsden, running around in a fleet of E20 vans.

The Ford Rally Team entered two BDA RS1800 Escorts for Colin Bond and Greg Carr. (Carr's the original English-built one but with new engine and extensively rebuilt, Bond's their new, Australian-built copy.) Their team's preparation was held up by an accident involving its ace mechanic, George Smith, [soon to become a valued member of the Datsun team] who was badly burnt in a pit fire at the annual Bathurst Hardie Ferodo race held the previous weekend. He could only provide consultation from his hospital bed.

The Holden Dealer Team entered only the one car and was considered lucky to even make the start, as the car, a 160bhp Gemini, was involved in a road accident only a few days before the event. Wayne Bell was the chosen driver."

From Tom's summary of the event: "Fury, and navigator Monty Suffern, swept aside all opposition to bring their Datsun Stanza home to victory in the 1978 Travelodge Southern Cross International Rally. Leading from the second section and without being headed, they dominated the event and finished without any major mechanical failures.

Colin Bond, expected to be Fury's main rival, experienced a few problems but nevertheless kept up the pace, but he and navigator John Dawson-Damer had to be content with second place after losing time on wrong roads and with several flat tyres.

George attacks a creek crossing at speed while Monty looks a little bored. Can you imagine?!

Although Bond on occasions could take fastest time on a stage, Fury widened the gap gradually. As the rally neared its end Fury's gearbox began to play up and he nursed the car over the last few stages." Fury/Suffern, first Australian winners for seven years!"

The inside story though, reveals it was not as simple as Tom's summary would have you believe.

For that story, I couldn't hope to better Pete Davis' account of the dramas preceding and during the '78 Cross, so here goes in his own words:

"FORTUNES OF THE CROSS (Written from memory and accuracy not guaranteed.)

It was a sight to behold; the car finally prepared and lined up in the workshop with all the Japanese works cars waiting to be loaded onto a transporter for Sydney.

Having suffered bad toothache for the previous week or so, I headed off to the dentist to have a tooth removed and gums stitched. Best to get it done before we leave I thought. More on that to come.

Arriving back at the workshop I was greeted with the sight of about six guys hanging in and out of the car undertaking significant work. Hey what are you doing to my car was the initial thought. How grateful I was when the scale of what was going on was disclosed to me.

George had thought it would be a good idea to give the car a final run along Governor Road, a local dirt road which was to become a major thoroughfare and industrial area in future times. We used the road often to give the cars a bit of a run. As we would have no opportunity in Sydney it was a good idea, and as it turned out a *very* good idea, which if not done, this story and a lot of history would not have been written.

During the test which was to be only a short run the tailshaft broke and ripped through the floor area, physically broke the gearbox, the very same one we had painstakingly built with loving care, and laid some internals on the road, the resulting shrapnel cutting into the seats. I believe it was only the solid construction of the seats built and supplied by Swampy Marsh, (yes the same Swampy Marsh from the film Odd Ball) that prevented injury to the crew.

So I come upon many people stripping the car, welding, sorting out spare gearboxes and a host of other jobs. Apart from our regular team we had a doctor and other part time crew who were there picking up service vans to drive to Sydney. What a great job they and all our team did – as the result of the Cross attests to.

As the transporter had to leave and our car was not ready it was up to Jamie and me to get the car ready and trailer it to Sydney. I can't remember what time we left or arrived in Sydney but we turned up at the motel underground car park and continued on with finishing the work started in Melbourne. I believe we were a few minutes late getting to scrutineering but suffered no penalty.

So all is good and off we go to Amaroo Park for the first stage. All of us feeling relieved but obviously apprehensive.

We had built a good rapport with the Japanese mechanics and engineers, and just as well. During our preparations we noticed that the spare differentials that had been sent out for the Cross had, we believed, a design flaw. We pointed this out to Mr. Shinoda, team engineer who turned an embarrassed shade, slapped his head and stated "not design fault but Japanese engineering mistake" it was pretty funny really and good to see we were not the only ones capable of cock ups.

We spent the next few days organising parts and machining to help the guys get the diffs up to spec. (we'd already done ours). They were very grateful which was to pay dividends later on.

So onto the first service and up in the air with the cars, each of us doing our own thing. For some reason one of the Japanese mechanics was under the mid-section of the car and I was under the back end. I'm not sure if he was helping because of our difficulties or whether he was scheduled to be there but no matter it was a rally saver.

The mechanic called to attract my attention and when I looked he had the gearbox drain plug in his fingers and it was on its last thread ready to drop out. Big smiles, thumbs up and a big thanks from me.

So, settling down, we just contended with the usual problems not least of which was the rear pads dropping out on 2 occasions. We could not work out what was going on naturally thinking we had made a mistake by not securing the retaining pins. It was very muddy and Bob Suffern, Monty's brother who was servicing with us, sorted it out. The Japanese in their meticulous attention to detail had joined the 2 very small retaining pins with a beautifully manufactured cable. This was to assist pad changes. If you were changing pads the clips would be easily seen and not lost in the panic. This normally worked extremely well but on this occasion the mud would build up under the cable and force the cable and pins to relocate to places unknown, resulting in the main pad retaining pins falling out and thus leaving the pads to depart company with the vehicle. Bob got onto this fairly quickly and it was fixed by simply cutting the cable. No loss of time thanks to George's driving skills."

I'll interrupt Pete's story for a minute here to give you Jeff Beaumont's great story of his and Rauno's engine failure and the drama that ensued, which occurred at about this point in the story:

"... I was again co-driving for the 'Flying Finn' Rauno Aaltonen but our run was short-lived as our engine spectacularly blew up early on the second night. Flames engulfed the front of the car while we were powering up an incline around the edge of a mountain. Rauno brought the flaming car to a quick stop while I undid my harness and grabbed the extinguisher. I quickly jumped out of the burning car... straight over the edge and rolled down the grassy slope! By the time I'd scrambled back up to the road, Rauno had exited the car and we dumped the contents of the extinguisher around the engine bay, putting out the fire. Bits of con-rod were hanging out of the block which obviously meant instant retirement from the event."

And back to Pete Davis:

"The drama was unfolding with the failing of the works Stanza's engines and Greg Carr suffering some sort of navigation or paperwork problem leaving us seven minutes ahead at the end of the first night. It was now our rally to lose with 4 days to go. That pressure was worse than being behind and chasing.

Action stations at Total service station Port Mac.

At rally midpoint the team would change all major components in the one hour allowed for service. This would include complete front and rear suspensions, gearbox, diff, clutch and anything else that was deemed appropriate to change. It was pretty good stuff seeing all this done in an hour.

This segment is a little hazy but I think we only did one diff change for the event. During the change it became apparent that I had made a mistake with the caliper brackets on the spare assembly (Australian engineering mistake) and their orientation was such that the banjo bolt holding the brake line to the caliper was interfering with the rear shock absorber on both sides.

Panic stations. Second last day, leading by 7 minutes or more and service time run out, what to do?

It was about 200km to next service so we filed the banjo bolt to give it what clearance we could and decided to swap out the axle caliper assembly from the recently removed diff housing and refit it to the car at the Wauchope service. This was a reasonably time consuming job and had to be done while all other service functions were completed. Enter Mr Gunn, one of the senior Japanese mechanics, asking what the issue was. We explained the situation, to which he replied "what do you want me to do?" 10 minutes tuition and we were ready to go. Car arrives, Gunn on one side, me on the other and everybody else doing their scheduled job.

The work was done and the car departed with us wondering if the old axle bearings would last the distance. 7 minutes in front, one day left to run, ours to lose!!

With much apprehension (and fatigue) we continue on into the night. We did the traditional, Div. 4 mid-stage service (The stage was 200+ kms. long and no time was allowed for the service). All good, tension and worry mounting. It's ours to lose. On our way to the next service we get the message over our radio network that George has no 2nd gear.

Has the failure of the tail shaft come to bite us again with the spare gearbox failing. I can't remember if the gearbox that failed in the car was a rebuilt unit or just a spare we had and had to use because we were short of boxes.

Fury and Suffern at speed in the NSW coastal forests

I don't think that was the case as there would have been spare boxes from the failed Japanese cars. But that's irrelevant. The issue is, do we have time in the service to change the gearbox? Nobody knows because ours is a bit different and difficult to change owing to our twin cam engine and we have never accurately timed a change. 7 minutes in front, ours to lose.

We drain the oil and determine that part of the 2nd gear synchro has failed and we have the broken bits to prove it. Smart heads from above prevail – Howard, George and Monty make the call to let it run as we think we have all the broken bits out of the box. The car holds together, much joy, tears and companionship with our Japanese counterparts follow.

For me, off to the dentist in Port Macquarie to determine why my mouth has been so sore since the tooth removal. Dentist removes a sliver of broken jaw a result of the tooth removal. A course of antibiotics and all is good with the world.

A great team effort and a great experience."

Final placings: Fury/Suffern first, down 1:25:17, Bond/Dawson-Damer second on 1:37:12, Bell/Shepheard third, on 1:58:32, and Dunkerton/Mortimer fourth, on 2:17:42. Fifth, Neale/Dodd, more than an hour further back.

To the winners go the spoils. 1st 1978 SCR

As a contribution to this book, Monty offered his story about the big part that luck played in their 1978 success:

"What's luck got to do with it? The story behind George Fury and Monty Suffern's 1978 Cross Win.

As any of us move through life, luck, either good or bad, is likely to have some influence on how things turn out. In motor sport in particular luck often affects the outcome. In 2013, Fernando Alonso, through no fault of his own, nearly had his head taken off in a spectacular first corner accident. Certainly, no level of driving skill could have changed the outcome from his perspective, although had he been lucky enough to be a couple of metres further down the track when the carnage came rushing up from behind, he might not have been involved in an accident at all. Who knows, he might have driven the rest of the race to some respectable podium place. But he wasn't and he didn't.

Sometimes in motor sport, missing out on the bad luck is nearly as good as having good luck. But for some, the saying "if he didn't have bad luck, he wouldn't have any luck at all" seems to fit well. For others, good luck seems to follow them around. In our rally career with the Nissan Motor Company, not many thought that George and I had any abundance of good luck. Rather than being followed around by good luck, sometimes all the luck you are going to get comes in one dynamite package. This story describes such an occasion. Some competitors manage to run off the road, flip onto their roof (which could be an event ending occurrence), then have the luck to see a couple of gorillas swing down out of the trees (whoops – profound apologies to those most important rally participants – the spectators), who push the car back onto its wheels, tell the navigator which way the other cars went (because he/she is still disoriented from the crash), and away they go – sometimes to victory. For us however, on the rare occasion we ever crashed, it was likely to be a four barrel roll down the road with no spectators in sight, and in any case, all four wheels had fallen off, so there was no point tipping us back off our roof (the last night of the Southern Cross in 1977 I think). However the 1978 'Cross set all that right.

The 1978 rally season saw the introduction of the mighty Stanza onto the Australian rally scene. We campaigned one for the ARC season with some success. It was a very good car operated by a very good and well managed team. Our thanks go to the mechanics and others who were so, so important in the successes of the year. For the Southern Cross that year, the parent Company in Japan sent the usual top notch team from Japan with two or three additional Stanzas for the international drivers who were coming for the event. All the final preparation of these vehicles was happening at the rally workshop in Braeside, a Melbourne suburb near Moorabbin airport. It was a regular beehive of activity, with not only the Japanese team members and our regular full time mechanics, but a number of other Australian mechanics hired by team manager Howard Marsden specifically for the Cross. From Braeside, the cars were to be loaded onto a car transporter for the trip to Sydney, ready for scrutineering and the start of the four day event. The transporter was scheduled to leave at 5:00pm for the overnight trip.

At about 3pm of the departure day, George sidled up to me and said to get in the Stanza as he was going to go for one last shakedown run in the car. This was suburban Melbourne, but there was a gravel road (albeit a very straight gravel road) a couple of km away. I was busy folding maps (or something similar) so I suggested he take my brother, Bob, who was one of the contract additional mechanics described above. Off they went, and about 25 minutes later there was a phone call for me (before mobile phones mind you), with George explaining I had better get one of the boys to come down with a trailer to Governor Road. This did not sound promising to say the least, but it was much, much worse than that. Seems that George had detected a small vibration in 5th gear and decided to see if it would 'drive through it' at higher rpm. So here they were, doing around 160 kph on a gravel road when the tail shaft broke, and all hell broke loose. At least we found out the small vibration was not just a figment of Geo's imagination. So part 1 of the "good luck" story was that the car was not pole vaulted end over end on the tail shaft hanging out of the diff. The car came back to the rally workshop on the trailer and the damage was assessed. To say this thing beat the shit out of the vehicle would not be an understatement. The shaft broke about 150 mm behind the gear box, and this short shaft flailing around tore the back off the transmission, but worse still, cut a 50 mm swath through the floor and the transmission tunnel. Shards of metal lodged in the roof of the car, all of which narrowly missed George's wrist as his hand was resting on the top of the gear stick in his attempt to "feel" where the vibration might be coming from.

The Japanese team looked over the car and said something to the effect of "stiff shit – looks like your car is out of the rally" (it was said in Japanese, so I did not get the exact wording). The Australian guys looked over the car and declared that we had a spare gear box and differential (in the service van ready to go to Sydney), and they could fix it, but it would take a while. The only concession made by the team management was that they would delay the departure of the transporter until 8pm, and if our car was on it, good for us. That meant something like about 3 hours – a piece of cake to a well-oiled rally team. Out came the seats; in went the oxy torches; and hammers beat things back into place. Strengthening pieces were welded in and painted over, shards were removed from the roof, mechanical components were put back in, and the car was on the truck to Sydney by the required time. [Memory is such a strange thing. I have accounts of this episode from both Jamie Drummond and Peter Davis who concur that the car was not completed in time to leave on the truck and they had to stay back to finish the repairs and then tow it to Sydney on a trailer. Outvoted I'm sorry Monty, I have to go with the majority on this detail.] *What a piece of teamwork with no apparent panic and with guys working all* over the car without getting in each other's way. And imagine what would have happened if the first time the car reached whatever critical tail shaft rpm caused the break, had occurred at close to 100 mph on a twisty gravel road just south of Newcastle on the first competitive stage. Frankly, I would rather not imagine such things. Thank you George for going on one last shake down run. So lucky break 2 has now been described.

"But wait – there's more", as the famous TV commercial proclaims. Good luck number 3:

The second night of the Cross was wet and muddy with rather treacherous conditions, and we were bombing along some twisty God forsaken mountain track (rally talk for a ripper road) when George says "no brakes". He probably said more than that, but there has been enough swearing in this story already. Turns out we had no brakes – no pedal at all. Well brakes only serve to slow you down (unlike "no steering"), so we pressed on to the end of the stage. As luck would have it, there was a service point up along the bitumen ridge road, but it was quite a few km up the "highway". Probably the Oxley highway, though my memory is not good on details, and my record keeping is even worse, so my chances of finding the route instructions after 35 years are non-existent. So we drive up there in the pissing rain with no brakes and one of the field vans is waiting for us with the two Bobs – Bob Woolley and Bob Suffern. Howard Marsden, the team manager, used to organise the service crews with the philosophy of putting the Japanese crews at the major service points where they could do what they do best (work very fast with well set up and well lit service points) and the Australians out in the field where they could fix things with a piece of string and a 3 inch nail. Well we needed more than a piece of string and a 3 inch nail but fortunately, our service van had the parts required to fix our problem, which was

George and Monty leading the '78 Cross – theirs to lose

to put new brake calipers on the rear of the vehicle.

The sequence of events happened like this: the pads were held in with two pins. For faster service, the pins were tied together with a fine braided wire so they could both be pulled out together (must save at least 3 seconds). Earlier in the year during the ARC events we had found that if mud packed under the braided wire, it would work the pins loose and the brake pads would fall out, so we removed the wire – problem solved. The Japanese mechanics noticed the wire was missing, so they put it back. In the muddy conditions of the second night, the mud packed under the braided wire, and the pins came out, followed by the brake pads, followed by the pistons (though I am not sure if they came completely out), hence the 'no brakes' comment from George. What I can say however is that everything was bloody hot, as brakes tend to be even when they are not working too well – I guess the pistons were in the calipers still. Bob and Bob burned the crap out of their wrists and hands changing these things, despite wearing gloves, but with nary a complaint to us. Including a quick field bleed – enough to get us going – it was probably less than 10 minutes or so for the whole repair. We did not even get out of the car (remember the pissing rain bit), and we lost no time on the transport section. Well done guys, and I hope we remembered to say thank you. Of course at the next major service point, while they were giving the brakes a proper bleed, the Japanese mechanics noticed the wire was missing and were in the process of replacing it, but someone pulled rank (thank you Howard), and the wires disappeared forever – well at least in Australian events.

The rest, as they say, is history. Our names are in the record books as winners of the 1978 Southern Cross Rally, a gruelling event of some 2730 km of which 1510 were competitive, including one stage of 205 km on the last night which included an "in stage" service for a couple of tyres and a splash of fuel (less than a 45 second stop). There were plenty of other long stages on other nights too, but the "long one" on the last night was always a mental and physical challenge. (Remember

Good to see Nissan getting its money's worth

the 4 barrel roll over when all the wheels fell off in 1977? Well that was on this long stage of the last night)."

The final part of Monty's story will be found in the 1980 Southern Cross report, coming up...

The Repco Alpine Rally – Nov 24-26, 1978 was not a round of the Australian Championship series and we'd not entered so I was able to run with Ian Swan in his 120Y as Car #26. Unfortunately, the off-side engine mount broke causing the oil filter to be holed and we lost oil pressure. This was one of only two of Ian's DNFs in an Alpine, I believe.

The Marchal Rally was held on December 17, after several postponements, in the gold-mining district around Ballarat, Victoria. The 1978 Australian Championship title rested on the outcome with Bond and Dunkerton starting the event each with 21 points and Carr and Fury each with 18. Any of the four could win.

After an event-long battle, Carr took the points and the title with Dunkerton placing second and Bond third, Fury retiring with another failed timing gear set. Carr and Dunkerton finished the year each with 27 points but Greg was awarded the title due to his three wins to Rossco's one. Colin took third on 25 and George fourth on 18. It had been an exciting year and one that had a suitably dramatic end. With the rally on a knife edge, Dunkerton set a blinding pace on the final stage but Carr was still a minute quicker. Pardon while I choke, but this was a well-deserved title.

Fury in the rather ill-fated Aaltonen '78 SCR Stanza at the 1978 Marchal Rally.

Dunko & Beauy second to Carr on count back for ARC

Tom Snooks said: *In the previous eleven years of the Australian Rally Championship, no series had approached the 1978 season for competition and drama. Never before had four drivers commenced the final round with a chance of taking out the title, and never before had the final result been determined by a tiebreaker!*

Apropos of what, I've no idea, but Rex Muldoon came up with a concept of making a movie dramatising his declared dream to drive a works rally car to Alice Springs. Somehow he was successful in convincing Howard of the idea's merit and it went ahead around the Christmas period. I'd be way too embarrassed to recommend the viewing of the resulting movie but I have a copy and it shows, among other banality, the Källström/Bilstam '78 Cross Stanza drifting on some dirt road around Ayers Rock. Not its finest moments.

Rex disappearing in his own dust

Monty's electronic rally meter built by friend, John Bailey, a forerunner to the TerraTrip.

1979

"At the beginning of the 1979 series it seemed unlikely that the drama of 1978 could be repeated. With each passing round though, it became clear that 1979 was to be a virtual repeat of the year before, once again going into the final event with the same four crews, Carr/Gocentas, Bond/Dawson-Damer, Fury/Suffern and Dunkerton/Beaumont able to take the title." Tom Snooks, 'History of the Australian Rally Championship'.

Round 1 was The Akademos Rally, our first event with new sponsor, AWA Clarion, and held in East Gippsland, Victoria. It began at Sale under threatening skies and soon delivered on the promise – most of the event being run in blinding rain and pea-soup fog. Watson (turbo Peugeot) and Portman 1600 Grunter were out early and by division end, Carr and Dunkerton were leading on 5 points with Fury on 6, followed by Bond on 7.

Dunko & Beauy starting ARC round 1

Division 2, with rain still tumbling, saw Fury take the lead and finishing on 20, then Carr and Dunkerton still tied on 22, and Bond falling behind – back on 29.

Ford's challenge collapsed in Div. 3 in which there were just two stages, 132 and 35 kms. Carr suffered with gear selection problems and dropped 7 minutes to Fury, and Bond had a brake banjo come loose, causing loss of brakes, to drop 46. In the long section the fog was so thick for 70 kms, cars were at times travelling at walking pace.

Fury/Suffern, winners of '79 ARC Round 1.

The Akademos was a great start to the season for Datsun with first place going to Fury/Suffern on 48 points and second to Dunkerton/Beaumont on 52 points. Carr/Gocentas were third on 66 points. Bond/Dawson-Damer finished fifth on 87.

The Rally of the West which started and finished in Perth WA was Round 2 for '79 and began in choking dust, changing to torrential rain and mud for two days.

At the very first service point it was discovered Fury's engine had very low oil pressure and, as we were unable to remedy this malaise, he and Monty were forced to retire.

Dunko and Beauy, a troubled run for third place in WA

At the end of the first night, Carr lead on 8 points to Dunkerton on 9 and Bond on 10.

Saturday's Div. 2 began with three short spectator stages and Carr was fastest on two and equal fastest with Bond on the other. They then went on to the longest stage – 130 kms, where Carr beat the time allowed by 5 minutes and Bond dropped 4 minutes. Dunkerton lost brakes with 100 kms to go and dropped 22. Still raining heavily, Carr had an off in the next stage and winched for 13 mins to get going. Driving at his best he managed to peg Bond back and finished the event just one point in front. Dunkerton a further 16 points behind.

So a big 1-2 for Datsun in '79's first round and a big 1-2 for Ford in the second!

From Pete Davis: *"I think in '79 we trailered the Stanza's to Perth behind the E20s. Pete Ryan was with us and we came back in convoy with Bondy's bus and the Ford guys. Very funny trip."*

This trip back was to be the most memorable part of the event for us. The Ford team got around the country in an old, stripped out bus that carried one Escort, all their spares etc, and trailered the second car behind. It also had a bed so bus drivers could be rested without even backing off the throttle. With our two E20s and trailers we had us a convoy and all of us had turns in each of the available seats and the bed. It was a raucous trip. The Ford boys had a toolbox on the throttle (pedal to the metal) and had their feet up on the dash while driving, there was singing and joke telling, load music from the tape deck and much frivolity. I can't remember how long the trip back to the east coast took but all three vehicles had big tanks and there wasn't much refuelling required even though it was reported the Ford bus used more than $2000 worth of fuel on the return trip! It was a great bonding exercise – we actually pinched one of the Ford guys later in the year. George Smith proved to be a significant influence on Team Datsun in several ways.

For The Castrol International Rally in 1979 we ran just the one car, now with the new sponsor boldly sign-written on the side. This was Harry Källström's '78 Southern Cross Stanza for George and Monty as Car #2, fitted up with George's engine. Carr had a mortgage on Car #1 in Canberra by this stage.

Fury/Suffern near Canberra but aiming for the moon!
Teddy Webber photo

George's engine didn't sound sweet though and we discovered he'd flattened the exhaust on a rock. After a hurried repair he soldiered on and was only 47 seconds behind Carr at the end of the daylight stages but with the daunting prospect of eating Greg's dust through the night. The engine was still not sounding sweet though and Portman was gaining seconds, soon taking over second place. Shortly after, the engine gave up the ghost and George and Monty had to retire with what turned out to be a burnt piston, no doubt as a result of exhaust back pressure.

Wayne Bell and George Shepheard had been very quick in the now turbocharged Gemini but its transmission couldn't cope with the extra power and they broke a gearbox. It was replaced in service with no time cost but later they shredded a diff which put them out. The other competitive crew was Geoff Portman and Ross Runnalls in the Autosport 1600 Grunter. If not for dust and a couple of instances of plug leads popping off, they'd have been right there hassling Carr for the lead.

Crews awoke on the morning of the final division to rain, meaning a combination of grippy and slippery roads and no dust! Carr began with only a four and half minutes advantage to Bond who had three and a half minutes on Portman. Geoff had the bit between the teeth and was determined to hunt Bondy down. True to his word he took 58 seconds off the Escort on the first stage, coming into control right behind him and putting Colin firmly on notice.

In the end Greg Carr and Fred Gocentas won with a seven plus minute gap to Colin Bond/John Dawson-Damer, just a minute or so ahead of Geoff Portman/Ross Runnalls who couldn't quite bridge the gap. It was Greg Carr's fifth consecutive Castrol International win.

The Lutwyche Village Rally in SE Queensland was yet another that began dry and dusty and turned very wet and slushy, such that the organisers had to work very hard with redirections to save the event.

There were lots of shenanigans by the boys in the lead-up that saw me at one point trapped out on the motel's balcony in my jocks – thanks boys – but this probably isn't the place to go into all that, so back to the story.

Carr once again set the pace and led at the end of Div. 1. Fury followed, then Dunkerton, Portman and Bond. Heading north after service and meal break, the skies opened and with the Escorts unable to match the Datsun in these conditions, pretty soon both Stanzas had passed Carr. Portman would have as well if not for a puncture. By Div. 2 end it was Fury by 1 minute to Dunkerton, then Portman, then Carr.

Before the rain. Dunko keen to show off the new sponsor.

After a delayed restart while organisers reshuffled the route to get around the worst of the rain affected roads, Carr attacked, trying to haul back the Datsun's lead, but dashed his chances with a puncture and then discovered he had no jack handle. Fury, being pressured from behind by his teammate, threw away what looked like another win when he arrived at a particularly slick bend. He was forced to choose between going straight on or hitting the bridge they were supposed to cross. The Stanza decided to go straight on. They ended up in a deep sided creek with nothing around to winch from. Such is the challenge of being first car on the road – while you sit there with wet feet, your warning triangles are slowing your competitors.

A forlorn scene greeted us when Pete and I reached them sometime just after dawn. We tried winching from the van's tow bar but the van wanted to go to the car rather than the desired vice versa. So we kept trying different parking spots til we found somewhere the van could sufficiently get its toenails into terra firma – nearly everywhere around was super slick. Once out, George was able to power away, amazing us with both his control and the rally car's superior grip, firstly in the direction we'd come in from and then, after apparently having a change of mind, blasted back past us and headed off in their original direction. We then had some hairy moments getting out of there with the van slipping and sliding around.

We met up with Jamie and Pete Davis on the way out. They'd come across a Datsun 1600 rally car broken down and needing a tow back to base and had him on a rather short tow rope behind their van. So two Datsun service vans followed very closely by a strangely quiet 1600 rally car headed off back toward civilisation at the only speed they knew. The guys in the 1600 probably had no idea that the van they were attached to was in radio contact with the other van they occasionally glimpsed ahead, and it must have been extra terrifying to be dragged over crests on the wrong side of double lines no matter how hard one pushed on the brake pedal. We all survived however, even though I'm sure those two blokes wished they'd pushed their car home.

Pete Davis sparked this memory for me: *"Do you remember us* [Jamie and Pete] *giving a crew in a 1600 rally car a tow down the mountain* [on a short rope!] *after they broke down. We were going like cut cats and the poor buggers were terrified not realising that you and Ryan* [Derek and Pete R] *were well in front telling us of oncoming traffic* [over the two-way]. *Very funny at the time but bloody stupid* [on reflection].

In the end it was Dunkerton on 36:56 with Portman next on 41:53, followed by Carr on 46:53. The result shot Dunko to the lead in the championship with 19 points to Carr's 17, Bond's 11, Fury's 9 and Portman's 6, with two events to go.

For The Bega Valley Rally in S.E. NSW, in a search for more grip, we took the Stanzas on wider 13" Hotwire wheels shod with 215 60 tyres. On the fast smooth roads in the Bega Valley though, these proved to be a retrogressive step and we quickly changed back to the gold Enkeis and 195 tyres on the front and soon

At Bega we reverted to 195x14 fronts at the 1st service and abandoned the 215s completely at the 2nd.

after, abandoned the idea entirely and went back to the 195s all round. Those Hotwires didn't see the light of day again until they were fitted to George's Stanza for the final two bitumen sections of the Motogard Rally in New Zealand.

Carr began quickly as usual with Fury, Bond and Dunkerton trying to stay in touch. At the first service we locked away the Hotwires and Carr had a troublesome diff replaced. Dean Rainsford, now in an RS1800 Escort needed to replace a damaged camshaft bearing!

Before the Div. Break, Bond was just 69 seconds ahead of Fury but then drama! Carr retired with distributor trouble, Portman with a broken drive shaft and Dunkerton had a high speed rollover but was able to continue to service and the meal break at Bombala. He arrived with front wheels on their own unique headings and the Stanza's bodywork in general disarray.

We were able to patch him up and must have improved the car in the process as he went out and set fastest time on the following section by almost 30 seconds to Fury. (Maybe it was the extra adrenaline.) There followed a hard night's rallying with the margins between Bond, Fury and Dunkerton ebbing and flowing but as they rolled into the finish at Bega that was how they'd finished – Bond 91:18, Fury 97.66 and Dunkerton 123.35.

Ross' Bega Stanza in it's new, faster configuration.

Third place here gave Dunko and Beauy the lead in the championship with just one round to go. Dunkerton/Beaumont on 23 points, Bond/Dawson-Damer had 20, Carr/Gocentas 17, Fury/Suffern 15, and Portman/Runnalls 5.

With memories of the previous year's disastrous Endrust Rally in SA, where we DNF'd three cars, this year's event started in the same vein with Fury, fastest in the opening three daylight stages, landed awkwardly from a high speed crest and slewed into a concrete pipe stanchion, which ended both his rally and his car's career in motorsport. Bond almost had the same accident and then, Paul Nudd with wife Barbara repeated it exactly in their 120Y.

At the Div. Break, Portman, 5:51 led Carr, 6:13, then Hugh Bell on 6:19, Bond on 6:28 and Dunkerton 6:35. After the break it was out into the wide open spaces and the rally proceeded at break-neck speed with Dunkerton getting into the lead but then puncturing, Carr taking a wrong road and losing two minutes and Bell retiring with a broken ball joint.

Dunko had to use Källström's SCR car for the Endrust in '79

At Div. end it was still Portman leading on 29:45 from Carr on 30:26 then Dunkerton on 32.23 and Bond on 33:39. Long time DRT helpers Chris and Simon Brown were running sixth on 38:17! Back in the forests, Carr was keen to make up the deficit and made it into the lead for a short while until a puncture put him right back again. He and Portman battled furiously to the finish with Dunkerton and Bond also locked in a tight battle for third. The Endrust finished with Portman and Runnalls' first ARC win, down 53:02 with Carr coming in behind them on 55.45 and followed by Dunkerton on 63:32 and Bond 63:57.

Dunkerton's third gave him sufficient points to win the 1979 Australian Championship for Drivers for the fourth time and Jeff Beaumont the Navigator's title for the third time. The final points tally for the year was Dunkerton/Beaumont on 27, Carr/Gocentas and Bond/Dawson-Damer equal second on 23 points each, and Fury/Suffern with Portman/Runnalls equal fourth on 15 points each. A brilliant and hard-fought series indeed!

We didn't have much to do with the **1979 Motogard Rally** in New Zealand but we did receive the two works Stanzas that had come first and second in Group 2. They were controversially disqualified from the results, so I've included that story here for context.

Timo Salonen, after several little problems including having his gear selector jam in second, had got himself up to second place at the finish. This pleased him immensely as it came so soon after a second placing on the Acropolis Rally. But his pleasure was short-lived. He must have been bitterly disappointed to be disqualified through no fault of his own. Another bitter pill was the fine of NZ$200 imposed on him by the stewards, as the driver of one of the affected cars.

After the rally the cars were put into parc fermé and teams notified they were to be subjected to a post-rally eligibility check. Salonen's Datsun had not only taken second place but had won the Group 2 category and was therefore required to be inspected. But Andy Dawson, team manager of Datsun Team Europe, as well as one of its drivers, told officials that he had been instructed by the Nissan company not to allow the cars to be stripped under any circumstances until they had arrived back at the factory. This final scrutiny requirement was clearly laid down in the regulations so the organisers then notified the stewards with a request that the stewards decide what course of action to take.

The next morning the stewards held an open meeting attended by Dawson, the organisers and other interested parties. Dawson repeated that he had been instructed not to allow the inspection of Salonen's car so the stewards brought in a prompt decision to disqualify the car from the results. Next highest in Group 2 was Dawson himself, so he was asked to submit his own car for inspection. He repeated his refusal and he too was disqualified. No appeal was made.

The obvious inference is that Datsun had something to hide. Dawson claimed that they (Datsun) wished to inspect the cars' engines before they had been touched by anyone else, but since they knew full well that successful cars are checked after major events, this seems a flimsy excuse. It's difficult to draw any other conclusion other than that the engines did not comply with the specs allowed under the regulations.

Three Stanzas arrived in Australia rather late before the Cross in '79 – two fresh from the Motogard in NZ that year and one from Japan. The accompanying crates of parts and tyres also arrived late so there was a scramble to swap engines and fit new components to the two Motogard cars and set the cars up for their respective crews. Both ex NZ Stanzas were immediately converted to Group 5 including new DOHC LZ engines – the Group 2 engines went straight into the crates the LZs had come out of, so I'm unable to shed any further light on the Motogard controversy.

Some of the required work was not completed before the cars had to leave for Sydney and there was a further scramble once we arrived there and even into the event itself as, from memory, new struts and gearboxes, listed in the Japanese schedule, were installed at service points. Not such a promising start in comparison to previous years' clockwork preparation... but who can say what constitutes winning preparation in this game?

THE STORY – 1979

The Southern Cross International Rally

Rather than reinventing the wheel, I'll again pinch a bit of Tom Snooks' *'History of the Southern Cross Rally'*. This from his 1979 event summary:

"Spearheading a magnificent 1-2-3 result for the Datsun Team, George Fury, navigated by long-time co-driver, Monty Suffern, took the winner's laurels for the second consecutive year. It was the third successive win for Datsun in the event, with Rauno Aaltonen winning in 1977.

Fury drove a consistently fast and careful event and had his equally consistent team-mates Ross Dunkerton/Jeff Beaumont and Rauno Aaltonen/Adrian Mortimer to finish immediately behind him. All in Datsun Stanzas.

But they had a mighty opponent in the Ford Team, comprising Colin Bond, Greg Carr and Bjorn Waldegard in the Escorts, with Geoff Portman running a Repco Reliability Trial Cortina.

The drama and excitement went on well into the fourth and final night, until Waldegard's Escort broke a differential four stages from the end, shattering Ford's hope of a win and leaving Colin Bond/John Dawson-Damer's Escort in fourth.

Lined up for the start at Amaroo, Bjorn Waldegard, Rauno Aaltonen, Greg Carr, Ross Dunkerton and Colin Bond! Dallas Dodger photo

From the outset, Waldegard showed his worth and Carr was the only driver who could stay with him in the early stages. Then the Fords were threatened from within when Carr's car retired after a broken axle and then a blown differential. From then on the Ford mechanics worked continuously on the remaining Escorts changing axles and the resultant time losses let the Datsuns stay within reach. Waldegard's Escort broke an axle on the second night but although not stopped by the incident it let Fury close the gap. Then, on the third night, after another broken axle, Fury took the lead.

However, on the last night Waldegard grabbed the lead back and was leading by a few seconds when the Escort's differential

failed (very likely because of the axle problems) and Fury was the winner again."

From the gala start in Sydney we all headed to Amaroo Park Raceway for the first stage – the usual feast for spectators. Dunko didn't let them down and performed a monster leap from the jump on the back straight, winning some minor award but also a good talking to by the Japanese management for threatening to end his event at the beginning of the first Division. Waldegard set the pace though with fastest time, followed by Bond, Carr, then the three Stanzas.

At end Div. 1, Waldegard had taken eight of the stages, Carr had been fastest once (by just one second) and Dunkerton once (by nine seconds). Positions were, Waldegard leading Fury by just over eight minutes, Fury led Aaltonen by almost one minute, who led Dunkerton by 1:40. Looking OK for Datsun considering the Fords' amply demonstrated frailty.

Dunko's prize-winning leap in SS1 at Amaroo Park in 1979

There were route difficulties at one point during Div. 2, leading to Waldegard going 15 minutes down a wrong road. Although the section was later deleted he was now well down the field and had considerable dust to contend with. At the end of Div. 2 it was Waldegard a little over six minutes ahead of Fury with about 1:40 to Dunkerton who had a bit more than four minutes on Aaltonen.

Again from Tom's book: *"This third division of nine special stages covering some 700 kilometres, took the course north through Kempsey, Bowraville, Bellingen and Coffs Harbour, then via the steep ups and downs of the Taylor's Arm area before returning to Port Macquarie.*

The top drivers were flying and the status quo remained until the fifth stage during which Waldegard dropped nearly seven minutes when a nut came off the front sway bar and he drove 90 kilometres with the damage, the last eight with a flat tyre. Fury dislodged a plank on a bridge and got through okay to be first at the end of the stage but his teammates were not so lucky. Aaltonen hit the loose plank and bent his rear axle assembly, and Dunkerton spun as he was crossing and hit a bank on the far side, also bending the Stanza's rear axle. Dunkerton's proved the quicker to fix and he lost four minutes – Aaltonen's took longer and he lost 36 minutes!"

Pete Ryan reminded me of the incident: "Derek and I and another of our chase crews, Jamie and Chris Brown, had been waiting for our cars just past the end of a stage near where the cars emerged from the forests not far from the hamlet of Taylors Arm."

George and Monty arrived there first! We checked all was OK and delightedly waved them on. We radioed the news in to Howard and waited. Rauno and Mort arrived next but things weren't so rosy. A bent axle from hitting something on a bridge. Jamie looked at changing just the axle shaft but it became obvious the housing was bent and he and Chris had to change tack (we almost always had a spare rear assembly ready to go in the vans.) In the meantime though, Ross and Jeff arrived with the same problem!

R to L, road positions in the Port Macquarie park fermé at start of Day 3, Fury, Bond, Dunkerton, Aaltonen, Waldegard.

By this stage Howard had also arrived (he and Rex Muldoon had set up their radio base for the night on a high spot somewhere nearby) so we had something of a traffic jam on top of a small crest in open farming land. As noted, Rauno's repair was taking some time and with that experience, Pete Ryan and I launched straight into changing the full rear end on Dunko's and he was away well before Rauno. As it turned out Ross got a brand new rear end and Rauno one that had been removed from one of the cars the previous morning at Port Macquarie – so much for privileged treatment for international drivers.

After service, and with his car repaired, Waldegard announced to his crew he would 'now attack' and proceeded to beat Fury by 41 seconds on the next stage, taking back the lead. He extended it further but then snapped an axle and lost several minutes. Dunkerton had a great night, –

fastest on three stages, second fastest on three, fourth twice and fifth once.

At Div. 3 end it was Fury/Suffern first on 14:33:56, Waldegard/Thorzelius second on 14:35:29, Dunkerton/Beaumont third on 14:42:21 and Aaltonen/Mortimer fourth on 15:33:56.

Waldegard had reclaimed his lead by midway through the second stage of Div. 4 when he passed George and Monty changing a flat tyre but he was not to go much further and blew a diff just up the road, leaving Fury/Suffern with a strong lead that they easily defended till the end.

Fury's winning margin was 14 minutes, 11 seconds to Dunkerton who was 1 hour, 4 minutes, 33 seconds to the good of Aaltonen and then a fast-finishing Bond/Dawson-Damer about 12 minutes further back. George and Monty had become one of just seven Southern Cross Rally winners, one of only three who'd won more than a single Cross.

George and Monty looking pretty happy about being two-time winners of the Southern Cross.

I can't now remember the thinking behind the decision, but for 1979 we'd chosen to run a wet sump on George's engine – maybe as a weight saving initiative? Mate, Dave Thompson, who'd been fabricating for the Holden Racing Team with Ian Tait, came in part time and made us two beautiful looking oil sumps with baffles and trap doors, all to combat surge in the large flat bottomed pan, and I built crank 'scrapers' to get the oil down into the sump. It didn't work as well as planned though and the engine breathed lots of oil from its crankcase vents which made for a messy under-bonnet and I needed to add oil at many service points. I wonder now (a little late) if we were maybe running the oil level a bit too high…

Not to worry, we'd won our second Southern Cross Rally and not just that – we'd again claimed the whole podium!

Aaltonen's Southern Cross Stanza was shipped to New Caledonia after the Cross where Dunkerton and Beaumont ran it in that year's

New Caledonian Safari. They had a huge crash in a transport section on a road Ross remembered from the previous year but which had been realigned. Rossco finished up in hospital with broken ribs, but the car was taken to the mortuary. (I've recently found out that in intervening years it has been brought back from the dead and remains in the Philippe Pentacost collection in Noumea.)

NC local with Jeff B. Ross in hospital

Back at Braeside we were joined by **George Smith** – recruited from the Ford Team. We were well advanced on a project to build a replacement for Fury's crashed ARC Stanza.

The project started with a new body shell from the spare parts warehouse just across the way (delivered by forklift ☺) and it was on-shipped to Talmalmo where George Fury began it with floor modifications and a roll cage. It then came back to Braeside to be finished, and under George Smith's influence it ended up lighter, stronger, and way better finished than anything we'd had before.

George's new Stanza before it's first event, the '80 WA ARC round. A head retension occasioning some topless action.

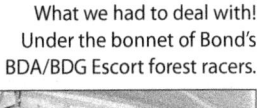

Les Collins, brilliant all-round engineer, great mate, go-to consultant to the rally team.

What we had to deal with! Under the bonnet of Bond's BDA/BDG Escort forest racers.

1980

Late February 1980 saw the final running of the Total Oil Economy Run, a sedate run from Sydney to Melbourne with two drivers and an on-board observer. Nissan entered a Sunny, a Stanza, a 200B and a 1 Tonne Ute. It was my job to prepare the vehicles and I had a lot of fun, shall I say, minimising the impact of the various emissions control systems on fuel usage. My reward for effort was to be No. 2 driver in the Stanza, alongside Ross Dunkerton

once again. We had a blast – lunch and overnight stops were a real hoot with all the motorsport and other celebs involved.

I remember Ross and I talking with one of the Honda cars crew who were doing really well with their economy in a model with a comparable engine size. We asked what driving strategy they were employing and they said, "we just drive it normally". After that we gave up on all the changing up at 2,500 rpm etc. etc. and just, 'drove it normally'.

At one lunch stop I remember Dennis Lillee throwing apples a prodigious distance to have them lob right beside people standing at lake's edge.

George Fury without the pedal to the metal

After the event the Stanza (dark green and registered ALF 676 and known for ever after as 'Alf') became my company car and then, maybe a year later was given to Geoff Portman who actually used it, in its near standard configuration, in a few events. It had quite a famous career.

While I was playing with Economy Run cars, we had Les Collins come in and fabricate some smaller aluminium flares for the Stanzas to replace the rather oversize fibreglass ones from Japan that we'd been using. We thought the smaller ones looked much better and we used these (with the odd repair or replacement) through to the end of 1981.

Getting down to something more serious, at the beginning of April, due to a transport strike, our two Stanzas were loaded up behind the two E20 vans and we headed off on the trip across the Nullabor to Perth for

The Rally of the West.

It was the first event for our brand new Stanza and both cars were looking striking in their new Total Datsun livery. It was at our motel, The Red Castle on the Great Eastern Hwy at Rivervale, that the great team photo I've used on the cover of the book, was taken with George F. more intent on something in the sky and new boy, George Smith (behind my left shoulder) looking rather sheepish. Maybe he was a little embarrassed about jumping the Ford ship and joining the opposition.

Setting out with small flares in convoy for Perth

The short story of the event was: Dust. So much dust that the organisers had to abandon after the last break and transport back to the finish as the field had become so strung out.

Dunkerton on the bitumen early in Div 1 near Perth

After the first daylight stages, close to Perth and including up the Zig Zag Scenic Hill at Gooseberry Hill, Bond as Car #1 took advantage of his dust-free run and set a scorching pace, only Fury able to keep him in sight. Carr had trouble with a failed distributor drive but soon after it was replaced, blew a head gasket and was out. At the first break it was Bond with an 18 second lead to Fury and then Dunkerton, seven-odd minutes adrift, his Stanza having a mysterious timing chain adjuster problem.

After the meal break Fury was consistently faster than Bond and soon hit the lead, while Dunkerton's timing chain adjuster broke and put him out. George and Monty held their position through to the next meal stop where the organisers discovered that some of the tail-enders still hadn't completed Division 1 due to the dust, and they decided to curtail and head straight to the finish.

The final scores were Fury in our brand new Australian-built Stanza, down 271:22, Bond next, down 275:54, then Clive Slater/Barbara Stubbs in a Toyota Corolla on 292:14 and Tony Masling/Brian Hope in their aluminium V8 powered Stanza on 307:47. Most crews looked pretty pleased to be stopping.

There was a rather dramatic (but funny looking back) event as we readied to return to Melbourne. Strike over, we were loading the cars and vans on a car carrier for the trip back east. The cars were on the top deck and we were trying to get the vans up onto the lower deck. Pete Ryan gunned ours and attacked the ramps and just as the front wheels passed the end of the ramps and were on the truck's deck, the ramps slewed sideways and collapsed leaving the van sitting on its towbar and pointing at the skies – a very wide-eyed astronaut Pete at the controls. I can't remember how we escaped from that dilemma, the rest of the story probably lost in laughter, but we must have. If only we'd had mobile phones with cameras back then :-)

Once again The Lutwyche Village Rally in Queensland was the second round, just one month but several thousands of kms away. Where the WA round was choked with dust, the Qld event was mired in mud and run in heavy rain, and in the end, it too had to be curtailed.

As well as the two Datsuns and two Fords, Bell/Shepheard in the Turbo Gemini, Portman/Runnalls in the Les Collins-built, Autosport 1600 'Grunter', fronted up at the start in Brisbane,

George and Monty doing the biz in a very sloshy Lutwyche

together with the other usual protagonists, Masling (Stanza), Mulligan (Escort RS1800), Slater (Toyota Corolla), Coote (Escort RS2000), Browning (Gemini), Vandersee (120Y) etc.

As was becoming the norm, Carr took the early lead on the way up to Nambour and was followed by Fury and Bond with Dunko losing a little as the result of an off. Portman/Runnalls retired with head gasket failure in Div. 1 and, at its end, Carr had a slim 9 seconds on Fury, with Dunkerton, Bond and Bell all within the next 2 minutes.

As Div. 2 began, Fury was taking time off Carr as the latter was having gear selection issues. The mechanism was changed at service but it had to be changed a second time when the replacement failed as well, costing seven minutes in transport and dropping them to fourth. Carr fought back to third by Div. 2 end – Fury, Dunkerton, Carr, Bond at this last break.

In the final division, with the rain still tumbling down, Carr managed to overtake Dunkerton for second but then the organisers were forced to abandon as several roads were now underwater. So final places were Fury on 236:54, Carr second on 238:19, Dunkerton third on 238:36 and Bond fourth on 244:22 – George and Monty's second win from two starts, 100% success with our new car!

Round three The Akademos Rally in Gippsland, Victoria, was thankfully not weather affected. Carr again took an early lead but soon had a puncture which he chose to drive on, causing some damage to the differential. It was checked at service but given the OK. On the following section however, for 60 kms he had drive to only one rear wheel so that, including the subsequent diff change, it lost them 40 minutes. Bond too had troubles, running off the road in Carr's dust and having to winch back on. Fury's engine broke a timing gear and he was forced to retire while leading.

Chequered Flag's centre spread from The Akademos

Then Dunkerton ran out of fuel! He and Beaumont just managed to push the car over a crest and then cruised six kilometres downhill almost to control, where a few spectators took over pushing duties and got them past the timing marker. Such was their lead at the time, Dunko and Beauy still managed to win by just over eight minutes. Bond/Dawson-Damer put in a steady performance, other than their one off in the dust, and were rewarded with second. Carr/Gocentas kept going this time and managed third, just under six minutes behind Bond and then Ferguson/Owers in their first run in the HDT No. 2 car, also put in a conservative effort and placed fourth, four minutes further back. Datsuns of Chris Brown (180B SSS) and Hugh Bell (1600) were fifth and sixth.

The fast shire roads around the south coast of NSW once again hosted The Bega Valley Rally on the Queen's Birthday long weekend in June. We ran three Stanzas for the first time here, Geoff Portman/Ross Runnalls getting their first and much anticipated full works drive.

At the end of the daylight sections on the first day heading south, Fury led by seconds to Bond and Carr who were locked together, then Dunkerton a few seconds back and another few seconds back to Portman.

In the early night stages, Carr took the lead but again struck trouble, this time with his alternator, dropping 15 minutes and allowing Fury back to the front, now well ahead of Bond. By division end at Bombala though, Dunkerton had taken the lead, 10 seconds to the good of Fury, with Bond well back in third and ahead of Wayne Bell (now with new navigator Dave Boddy) in the Turbo Gemini, then Portman. Missing was Carr/Gocentas who'd had a fan belt jump off and take the timing belt with it (sounds to me probably related to the alternator change). In the last few stages of the night Fury took some seconds off Dunkerton and regained the lead, other positions remained unchanged.

Out in the scrub but still cool – Portman & Runnalls at Bega

In Sunday's daylight stages Bond was trying very hard and took a minute off Fury and even more off Dunkerton so that, at the Narooma meal break, Bond had slipped into second ahead of Dunkerton who was suffering rear brake problems. Bell/Boddy didn't get to eat as they got stuck in a creek crossing and could not restart the engine. And so the event wound down, with Bond trying hard but unable to breach an eight minute gap. Fury won on 6 hours, 19 minutes, 43 seconds, less than one minute ahead of Bond in the end, Bond on 6:20:20. Next was

Dunkerton/Beaumont on 6:20:56, then Portman/Runnalls on 6:31:25 after an uneventful first works run and followed by Ferguson/Owers in the second HDT Gemini on 7:08:52.

With one round to go, Fury/Suffern led the title tally on 27 points to Bond/Dawson-Damer on 21. If Fury/Suffern could place third or better in the last round, the 1980 ARC would be their first outright title...

With the withdrawal of the Endrust Rally from the ARC for 1980, The Donlee Rally again stepped up to the plate as the South Australian round, even though based in Broken Hill in NSW, on the wrong side of the border. Although Broken Hill is just a gentle thirteen and a half hour drive from Bega (following the NSW/SA/Vic borders) the difference in terrain could not be more stark.

On parking duty in Broken Hill, George Smith looks across at his ex boss from George Fury's seat.

Desert surrounds Broken Hill with fast but rough roads, plenty of deep potholes full of bull dust and few trees to define the tracks – a nervous place to try and lock up a championship.

Teams were briefed – Ian Hill was given some works support with his Escort RS1800 and he and Carr needed to support Bondy to win by doing their best to grab second and third places. Fury had to drive a conservative event, Dunkerton and Portman needed to go for it and keep Bond from winning. Chris and Simon Brown joined our service crew, driving a semi-prepared Stanza and would try to wait for Fury/Suffern at every finish control to cover any mishap. And so it began...

At the first break, Carr led by 14 seconds to Portman with Bond third, just 4 seconds ahead of Dunkerton. Service crews were working hard to repair damage from the rough terrain. After the break however, Ford's plans began to implode. First Carr retired with a failed gearbox (one of the Escort's Achilles heels) and then Dunkerton with an engine issue (of which I can't remember the details). At division end it was Portman in the lead by some seven minutes to Bond who was around two minutes ahead of Fury, doggedly but cautiously hanging onto third place, despite having damaged both rear quarter panels and bending a rear axle housing! Luckily this time, he and Monty were close to service and apparently we changed the rear end in 13 minutes, ensuring they lost no time.

At the beginning of Division 3, Ford's strategy was in tatters with Carr/ Gocentas out and Hill/Heaney having missed a passage control. All Bond could do was hope Fury would fail. For Datsun though backup plan B was holding. Portman, with the dust-free run, pulled further away from Bond and Fury stuck to the back of Bond's thickest dust. As it wound down, Portman slowed more and more to make sure of his win. Final scores were Portman/Runnalls on 5:53:47, a little over seven minutes to the better of Bond/Dawson-Damer on 6:01:07 and Fury/Suffern 4:22 further back on 6:05:29. Fourth place, locals Gary Burns/David Milne in their Datsun 1600, were more than half an hour behind Fury.

Fury trying to dodge the bull-dust holes in the '80 Donlee

Our cars won all five rounds in 1980, three to Fury/Suffern and one each to Dunkerton/Beaumont and Portman/Runnalls. Notably though, at the end of this year's series in which Colin Bond had finished second in four events and fourth in the other, he had set the incredulous record of consistency in finishing every one of the 16 ARC rounds over the past four years – never in lower than fifth place!

Fury and Suffern fourth in the 1980 Motogard Rally in NZ
Dave Wood (NZ) photo

Following Fury's wins in the '78 and '79 Southern Cross Rallies, plus his 1980 ARC title, he and Monty were rewarded with an invitation to the Motogard Rally in New Zealand to drive one of the works Stanzas (or 160Js as they were called over there) alongside teammate, the new international Nissan-contracted hot-shot, Timo Salonen. It proved a great opportunity for George to measure himself against a quality international field and he did well and finished fourth, following home Timo Salonen, Walter Rohrl, and Hannu Mikkola. Björn Waldergård placing fifth behind George.

George's NZ car was smartly shipped to Australia after the Motogard for Geoff Portman and Ross Runnalls to run in the 1980 Cross – reward for supporting our team so well at the Donlee.

The Southern Cross International Rally

By 1980 The Southern Cross was well and truly in its death throes, The Australian Sporting Car Club was in financial trouble, the event administrators had stepped down, and it could not attract a major sponsor. Just eight weeks before the start of the event CAMS organised a rescue with Castrol Rally Director, Geoff Sykes in charge of the route and assisted by NSW CAMS Manager, Peter Reynell. Some sponsorship was scraped together from The Port Macquarie Chamber of Commerce (or similar) and Travelodge. Even if they could get the 1980 SCR completed it was hard to see how there could possibly be one in 1981 unless something near miraculous occurred.

Looking good here but George had a spin soon after

Only 45 entries were received and 44 of those started, headed by Ari Vatanen/David Richards in Colin Bond's Escort RS1800, which was converted to LHD for the event – Colin focussing on the Team Manager role.

Car #2 was George Fury/Monty Suffern in our Australian-built Stanza. Car #3 was Greg Carr/Fred Gocentas in the second works Escort RS1800. Car #4 was Ross Dunkerton/Jeff Beaumont (Jeff's twelfth Cross) in the Stanza in which they'd placed second in '79 and campaigned hard during the 1980 ARC series. Car #5 was Geoff Portman/Ross Runnalls in the Stanza that Fury had driven in the Motogard. Car #6 was Wayne Bell/Dave Boddy in the once again non-turboed HDT Gemini. Car #7 was Bob Watson/Wayne Gregson in the VW Golf that Cowan had run in the '78 Cross. Car #8 was Ed Mulligan/Phil Bonser in an Escort RS2000, and Car #9 Ian Hill/Anne Heaney in another RS2000. Car #10 was the first Japanese this year, Nobuhiro Tajima/Kioshi Kavamura in a works assisted Stanza.

Notably, for 1980 the Japanese Datsun works support crew stayed at home, for the first time leaving responsibility for service and organisation to our Australian team.

This was not the longest or toughest Cross – 2,600 total kilometres, 1,100 competitive, four stages over 100 kms, the longest, 138 kms on night four – but it made up for this with drama, with five leaders and a final night full of carnage. Dunkerton moved from fourth at end day 1, to third at end day 2, to second at end of day 3, and finally first when the chequered flag fell – a perfect strategy for a 4-day event.

On day one, after the usual flag away from Hyde Park, Sydney, cars headed to Amaroo for the traditional spectator extravaganza. This time the 4.4km stage was run twice, the second time in reverse, as stage two. Carr was just one second faster overall than Vatanen, who'd had a half spin on the first run. Portman was third fastest then Dunkerton, Bell, Fury, who'd also had a moment on the first stage, clobbering a bank and stopping for a second or two.

In the longest section of Div. 1, not far short of Port Macquarie, Vatanen was 16 seconds faster than Portman followed by Dunkerton then Fury. Carr had brake problems and a flat, losing three minutes. Then Vatanen had his first of several mishaps of the event where a sticking throttle (allegedly) caused him to SO into tree, but was able to continue with some body and suspension damage. Bell in the Gemini was delayed by a broken ignition wire that dropped them to 26th by division's end. Watson, not enjoying the Golf, was placed 25th at Port Macquarie.

Dunkerton, Fury, Portman in park ferme at Port Macquarie

End Div. 1 saw Vatanen leading on 96:38 to Portman on 97:07, Fury on 97:45, Dunkerton on 98:14, Carr on 100:38 and Hill/Heaney on 106:48

Div. 2 headed south and west and initially Carr was fastest, Vatanen suffering a seized strut which slowed him somewhat. At Taree meal break Vatanen was nine seconds to the good of Portman who had 37 seconds over Fury who had a minute on Dunkerton. Somewhat mysteriously, Carr was a further almost three minutes further back, but then, soon after lunch, he lost another eight minutes with a broken fan belt and Vatanen 11 minutes with a failed alternator. Dunkerton also had trouble – a broken rear shocker and two punctures. Wayne Bell was outed by another blown head gasket and Watson by a broken gearbox.

Portman and Runnalls were flying until the weather turned

Portman was now flying – much quicker than the other top runners. Vatanen then had a sway bar come loose, dropping another four minutes. Come dawn, back at the Sandcastle, it was Portman on 318:53 leading Fury on 320:24, then Dunkerton on 328:00, and Carr on 331:31 Vatanen still in the picture on 332:20 but Hill was losing touch on 348:41.

Div.3 headed north to Coffs Harbour and back. Vatanen was setting the pace but then the weather changed and so did Portman's luck. He flew over a crest but caught a protruding log causing a broken tension rod. Repairs cost 30 mins putting he and Runnalls back to sixth and allowing Fury into the lead and Dunkerton to third. Carr had an off, going backwards into a bank, and then the engine wouldn't restart until the penny dropped for Freddie Gocentas who was able to free the clay from exhaust tail pipe and allow them to continue. The Fords had further trouble with Vatanen going off and damaging the front end – again, costing them 12 minutes and Carr losing front brakes for a stage, costing them two minutes odd. Out in front, Fury and Dunkerton advanced their positions, Dunko despite battling a sticking throttle. When times were tallied back at Port, Fury led on 543:36 to Dunkerton 550:48, then Carr on 557:17, Vatanen on 585:50, Hill on 595:59 and then Portman sixth after a shocker on 601:00.

We changed Ross' carburettors before the restart on Day 4, expecting (in vain) to cure his sticking throttle.

Just 27 crews started Div. 4 which headed west then south to Wingham and Taree then returned to Port Macquarie for the finish. This was maybe the toughest division and contained the longest stage. Ford's horror continued when Carr again lost all brakes and hit a bank, bending his front end, and with one wheel facing the wrong way he quickly demolished its tyre. Apparently he and Fred had changed the flat but the replacement soon suffered the same fate. This led to a memorable moment for Pete Ryan and myself as Greg stormed out of the stage end, where we and his own chase crew were waiting. In less than a sweet mood, rather than stopping there for help, he tore up the highway with bits of rubber and sparks flying.

How not to win the 'Cross

At some point up the highway the wheel running on the road locked up and by the time they arrived at service, a good part of the wheel, the brake disc and the ball joint were missing. He lost another seven minutes on this transport section as his crew had to fit another strut assembly, straighten the steering to get the wheels facing in the same direction, and fix the brakes.

The photo of the strut removed at that service has been reproduced a number times already and with a few different captions, one of which I thought rather appropriate for Greg – 'there are no tomorrows'. Such a great driver – if only he'd been able to keep his emotions in check...

Ford's miseries were no doubt salved somewhat when news came through that Fury was out with a catastrophically blown engine, leaving Dunkerton with a 14 minute lead over Carr. This must have spurred Greg as he proceeded to take three minutes from Dunko in the next section – Vatanen, running second on the road, was frustrated in Dunkerton's dust. Then came the 138 km section...

Firstly though, this seems like the appropriate time to conclude Monty's story about luck, from the 1978 event so please excuse this small interruption:

"If you ever hear of me complaining that if it wasn't for the bad luck, we wouldn't have any luck at all, just remind me of the tail shaft incident on Governor Road, Mordialloc, and the brake caliper change up on the Oxley highway (or wherever it was). I'll try to be contrite. On the other hand, perhaps I will recall the start of

the last night of the 1980 Southern Cross Rally, which we were leading comfortably when the engine blew up big time just as we finished the first competitive stage of the evening. On disassembly of the engine (using a tension wrench) Geo found that two crankshaft main bearing bolts were not much more than finger tight. So I guess that can hardly be called bad luck. It is likely that some little engine builder back at the Nissan factory in Japan fell on his sword over that one.

I suppose I should be recalling the good luck we had in even getting to the last night given the circumstances, or better still that the engine quit just as we passed the timing marker at around 7pm, so we did not have to walk a long way out of the stage in the wee hours of the morning in the freezing cold, as had happened more than once before, and we could get back to the Sandcastle before the bar shut."

Back to the main story: Shortly after the start of the long one, Portman's engine died suddenly as yet another Japanese timing gear set failed. Dunkerton too was having trouble, the sticking throttle and ignition cutting out momentarily forcing him to drive on the ignition key and suffer a stuttering engine.

Carr's Escort had accidentally left service with one 13" and one 14" wheel on the rear, causing handling problems and to make matters worse he had only two soft compound spares on board – good for just 30 kms!

As a result the long stage became a procession of the walking wounded – Dunkerton turning the stuttering engine off when he had to brake and both Carr and Vatanen arriving at the end with completely bald tyres. Carr had managed to take 10 minutes off Dunkerton's lead however, leaving just a slender three minutes to protect.

Jamie has an amusing but somewhat disconcerting story about this section, so in his words…

"…*Howard and Rex* [Muldoon – assisting HM with service planning and mapping] *sent me and George into the middle of the stage to sit in this cutting on a long corner! Anyway Ross got through no worries! But on the way into that point we went down hills that there was no way we were going to get back up to get out that same way! So George and I made an executive decision! To follow a rally car after 1 min! So we did – it was an Escort. We caught and passed it in no time, so we were committed to going hard for the rest of* the stage, there was a lot of downhill and the brakes had started to disappear!

Then we popped out of the forest and there was a bloody spectator point at a creek crossing!

I remember hitting the creek and the old van got airborne (bloody high). Then there was a T junction – rally cars went right! I did this big flick and went left! Luckily the spectators parted!

George and I were so relieved [to be out]."

Easing the pressure, for us anyway, Carr suffered yet another puncture in the following stage and dropped 23 seconds to Dunkerton. With just two stages to go, if Ross and Jeff could keep it all together, they'd win. And they did.

The final scores were Dunkerton/Beaumont, victors on 836:26, Carr/Gocentas second on 839:26, Vatanen/Richards third on 863:29 and Hill/Heaney fourth on 898:52. Ross' first Cross

A tired looking crew picked up more than a trophy

victory in his lucky seventh Cross and Jeff's second in his 12th!

Datsun had been represented in all but the first run Southern Cross in 1966. They'd had class wins in 1967, '68, '69 and '70 and then placed fourth outright or better in every Cross after that, apart from '73 where Kilfoyle only managed sixth.

We were able to slip in a replacement engine so George and Monty could run their Southern Cross Stanza in the The Alpine International Rally in north east Victoria the following month. The LCCA (Light Car Club of Australia) received 103 entries for the event and most of Australia's best tackled the forests around

Fury/Suffern good enough for 4th place in a star-studded Alpine

the town of Bright and the Ovens River Valley. Ford ran the two RS1800 Escorts for Carr and Bond, Datsun ran just Fury, with Portman back in his Autosport-sponsored Datsun 1600. Long time Datsun Rally Team helpers Chris and Simon Brown started as Car #7 in Chris' 180B SSS.

Carr had a resounding win, consoling him somewhat for his Southern Cross miseries. Portman showed that old Datsun 1600s never die, beating Bond to second place by just two seconds and Fury was nearly two minutes further back in fourth.

In something of a return to rallying career roots, yours truly navigated in Car #38 for old friend and Datsun Sales Centre, New Car Sales Manager, Bruce Wilson. We had a steady run placing 28th of the 81 finishers.

As Dunko's reward for his Southern Cross victory, he was lent our spare Stanza and it was flown to Port Moresby to run in the PNG Safari - Dec. 12-15 in 1980. I was asked to navigate! What a great adventure – and so many funny stories. Suffice to say that we led the event by a good margin for three days until I mis-plotted the last control on the last night – a transport to get us back to Port Moresby – and we spent 40 minutes driving around the airport hunting for the missing control. I went to bed in disgrace. There was only a spectator stage to do in the morning and it would be over. Ross wasn't happy and took out his wrath on the car – the DOHC engine dropped a valve, ending our event. Thinking about it now, I reckon he knew best how to take revenge on the engine man.

All smiles before the start of the 1980 PNG Safari

And so ended 1980, it felt like the end of an era particularly as both Ford and Holden had announced they'd not be continuing in 1981, The Southern Cross Rally was almost certainly finished, and we were fresh out of serious competition. We'd played a big role in what became known as the 'Golden Era of Rallying in Australia' and had won everything to be won. Howard had another trick up his sleeve though that would get us another year of fun in the dirt.

1981

Howard's' plan for 1981 involved the promotion of the newly released Stanza SSS (which happened to coincide with the world-wide dropping of the Datsun name for passenger vehicles) by running cars very closely resembling those available from the showroom floor in the Australian Rally Championship, including the use a reasonably standard-looking L20B engine.

Portman/Runnalls, all conquering in 1981

1981 would be a transition year for rallying in Australia as CAMS intention was, for 1982, to move away from the near open-slather Group G class and toward the more standard Group A class, although what was to arrive was actually PRC (Production Rally Cars). The hope was to attract car company support once again, but sadly the strategy didn't work and, looking back, the transition was to be from a 'Golden Era' to the doldrums.

Nissan had their sights on another category of motorsport however, and our transition to circuit racing also served to mark the company's dropping of the Datsun name and the introduction of the Nissan Bluebird. But first we have a rallying story to complete.

Dunkerton's works drive was downgraded for the ARC year to, 'here's a car but you'll have to get it to events and support it yourself'. His 1980 Stanza, along with his works driver status, was given to Portman, and Dunkerton was given Portman's 1980 Cross car. It was a difficult year for Ross with Marsden doing his best to have him exit the team, giving him second rate equipment and even asking him (in Queensland) to take a dive to allow Portman to win – threatening to withdraw the car mid-way through the event if he wouldn't comply. In Ross' own book, *'Dunko – The Inside Story of Ross Dunkerton, an Australian Rally Legend"*, he has confused 1980 (one of his best) and 1981 (one of his worst) and covers both as just one year – a shame to taint his Southern Cross winning year with memories of being forced out of the Datsun team.

So, as a beginning to what would be a very busy year, the first round of the Australian Championship, The Rally of the West was run in

THE STORY - 1981

WA on the Easter weekend of Apr 17-19. Howard had deigned to send a SOHC-engined Stanza across to Perth for Ross and Jeff to run, albeit at their own cost.

Dunkerton, with his own business as sponsor, first in WA

It began with the usual spectator stages in the Southern suburbs of Perth on Good Friday and the local, Bob Nicoli (a name you'll have seen elsewhere in this book), was quickest in a Datsun 1600 followed by Clive Slater (another local) in his Toyota Corolla. Dunkerton was next, coming to terms with the unfamiliar and lower-powered Stanza. Just before the meal break its clutch failed but little time was lost and it was changed at the meal break. At end Div. 1, Nicoli had five seconds on Mulligan (Escort RS1800) who had nine seconds on Dunkerton.

On the Saturday morning stages Dunkerton was still off the pace but after lunch, began to fight back. The pressure was apparently too much for Nicoli who slid off and was stopped for several minutes allowing Dunkerton and Slater's Corolla through and dropping to third. Dunkerton/Beaumont went on to win with a score of 262:41 to Slater/Van der Straaten second on 263:50 and Nicoli/MacNeal third on 268:24. It was later learned that two other Stanza drivers had received financial support from Marsden for the event but unfortunately neither of them featured in the results.

For The Castrol International Rally in March, as a pointer to where our team's future lay, Jamie prepared a set of much lower suspension for George's Stanza to run the early bitumen stages. We also took along a set of Globe Bathurst alloy wheels fitted with slick racing tyres.

Though no longer running under Ford's banner

Fury unbeatable on the bitumen near Canberra.

Once more down the mineshaft

and colours, Greg Carr and Fred Gocentas appeared in the RS1800 BDG Escort, now painted white with Castrol stripes and signage, as Car #1 (as usual) and Fury/Suffern were Car #2. Wayne Bell was there as Car #8 in the HDT Gemini, now with an Isuzu 2-litre twin cam engine, and also in Castrol livery. Sadly but not unexpectedly the Gemini didn't last long and retired with no oil pressure before dark.

Fury beat Carr's times on the bitumen by a total of 20 seconds but, by the beginning of the night sections, George and Monty led by just four seconds. Sometime in the night Carr's gearbox began giving trouble and not long after, they were out. This left George only to protect his lead from Hugh Bell in his quick 1600, Chris and Simon Brown in their also quick 180B SSS and Ed Mulligan/Geoff Jones in an RS1800 Escort. It all fizzled out with Hugh Bell taking a few seconds off Fury's times on most stages on the second day, when what he needed was minutes. We didn't need to refit the race suspension for the later bitumen sections and George and Monty quite easily took the win by about four minutes – very happy to finally be standing on the top step of the podium in Canberra.

The Lutwyche Shopping Village Rally, out of Brisbane, Queensland, was again the second round of the ARC and held on the weekend of May 3-4. We entered Fury/Suffern as Car #1 still with a twin cam motor and Portman/Runnalls with the SOHC L20B motor as Car #3. Dennis McGreevy Datsun (a local Qld. dealer) entered Dunkerton/Beaumont in Portman's cast-off Stanza as Car #2. Once again Hugh Bell/Steve Ellis in their 1600 and Ed Mulligan/Geoff Jones in an RS1800 Escort looked like the only other crews capable of matching the pace at the front. Thankfully there was no rain to mar the event this year.

As usual the 'Lutwyche' began in Brisbane and headed north to some daylight stages in the Beerburrum forest, following which, Fury had a slender lead to Portman and Dunkerton. At the first break, Dunkerton had moved ahead of Portman and Fury/Suffern who had sufffered an uncharacteristic drive up a wrong road losing eight minutes.

In the second division, Fury set the pace and was fastest on all but one of the night stages, but not able to make up the deficit. At this point, Marsden approached Dunkerton and asked him to slow and allow Portman to win. Ross says he initially refused as he was paying the bills but Marsden countered, saying he'd withdraw the car from the event if Ross didn't co-operate. Dunkerton was forced to concede but insisted Fury be commanded to hold station in third.

Denis McGreevy Datsun assisted Ross and Jeff in Qld.

Portman moved to just over a minute ahead of Dunkerton. Hugh Bell and Tony Masling (aluminium V8-powered Stanza) now separated Fury from third and he'd just resigned himself to settling for fifth when Bell ran off and crashed out, and then Masling ran off and didn't have a winch to get back on!

The event wound down without further change to the top places and Portman/Runnalls ran out winners on 5:15:31, Dunkerton/Beaumont 80 seconds back on 5:16:52, and Fury/Suffern nearly three minutes back on 5:19:47. The team rancour worsened at the presentation dinner when, as Ross tells, Fury approached him and insisted he have the second place prize money as he'd forfeited second place to him. Apparently he told George to go jump, or something similar. Ross says in his book *"I'd never even thought to ask Howard for the first place prize money..."*

The Bega Valley Rally in NSW was held over the usual Queen's birthday weekend of June 14-16. Nissan had entered Portman/Runnalls and Fury/Suffern and again Dunkerton/Beaumont were entered by Queensland dealer, Denis McGreevy Datsun. Fury was a no-show however, as his Stanza had been damaged in a mishap in a 'learning race' on bitumen at Amaroo Park Raceway the previous weekend.

In the first division north to Merimbula, Portman and Dunkerton cleared away from the field and at the lunch break, Portman led by a little less than two minutes but after lunch, on the way back to Bega, there were several withdrawals including Dunkerton whose differential failed mid stage, and Hugh Bell who hit a bank and was not able to continue.

Chris and Simon Brown in their 180B SSS went to third place behind Wayne Bell, this time in a Holden Commodore.

Portman backed right off in Div. 3 and cruised to victory while several others, still contesting hard, came to grief. Back at Bega there were exactly half of the 66 starters still running. Portman had won on 4:31:22, to Wayne Bell on 4:41:13 and Chris and Simon Brown on 4:43:06.

Portman/Runnalls moved to 40 Championship points, Dunkerton/Beaumont remained on 35.

Try as the organisers might to make that year's Akademos Rally special for both competitors and spectators – it being the last time it would be part of the ARC – the event turned out to be a big disappointment.

Rosco turfed out for George. Who is Orient Auto Scene though?

Run on the weekend of August 29-30, most of the NSW crews opted to instead enter the conflicting 2WS Stadium Rally Challenge at the Sydney Show Grounds which offered good prize money. Sadly, the Akademos was poorly attended and had several long breaks intended to provide spectators time to assemble at the next viewing point. They also endured periods of heavy rain – pleasing no-one. Also, as George's Stanza still hadn't been made ready after his crash in a sports sedan race at Amaroo Park, Howard ejected Ross from the team and gave his car to George for this event. This was troubling as Ross had a first and a second in the ARC to that point to George's solitary third.

Night fell as crews headed for Sale in East Gippsland and, a few stages in, a particularly bad corner caught out nearly the whole

Those I can ID here, from left: Steven Kaitler, Lisa Portman, Peter Anderson, behind Anne Collins, Geoff P. (drivers seat) Phil Rainer, and myself checking the fuel level.

field (Portman excluded) with Fury collecting front guard and door damage but Hugh Bell collecting a DNF when he was unable to continue.

Portman cruised to an easy victory, 2:46:13, two minutes plus ahead of Fury/Suffern on 2:48:22. (Fury had been given Dunkerton's single cam car for the event) Wayne Bell/Col Parry in the Commodore were third nearly ten minutes back and the Browns fourth, a further one minute down, in their 180B SSS. This result gave Portman a huge and unassailable lead in the Championship with just the Alpine Rally to go.

Maybe as a consolation for having to give up his car to Fury for the Akademos Rally, Howard entered a Stanza for Ross and Jeff in The Macleay 1000 off-road race on the southern border of Queensland on the weekend of July 18-19. My brother John and I went as service crew, towing the car up in convoy with the Portman crew, Geoff, Phil Rainer (co-driver), Lisa and Twigger.

Dunko & Beauy practicing low flying for the Macleay 1000.

Ross drove a brilliant race and brought the Stanza home straight in second place to Australian off-road champion Gary Baker, in his purpose-built buggy. Geoff also did very well placing third outright in the 1600 Grunter. A great showing by the rally fraternity.

Before that though we had one other event to attend. Other than rally car preparation, much of 1981 was spent in the Braeside workshop converting a standard, off-the-showroom-floor, independent rear end (IRS) Bluebird Turbo into a race car. Looking at the competition in the 4-cyl classification for Australian Touring Cars (in '81 classes were determined by the number of cylinders), the powers that be must have thought we had some sort of chance of a class win at Bathurst. As it turned out, the Japanese prepared sister Bluebird (which arrived at Braeside sometime shortly after the Akademos Rally), running max. boost, despite heavy rain and high wind, qualified first in class and 31st outright. Our locally built car qualified fourth in class and 43rd outright. But I'm leaping ahead of myself.

Pete Anderson and I pretending to be hard at work on Bluebird #2

I can't remember too much about the preparation other than what I see in this posed photo taken at Braeside of new team member Peter Anderson (yes, another Pete) and I, dismantling the new road car.

Another photo reminded me of testing days out at Calder Motor Raceway, of which there were several. In the photo I have, George is stepping out of the car and everyone looks very serious so I guess we weren't happy with something. Howard is there with a journo in tow, Fred Gibson is leaning on HM's Skyline in the background, thinking what, I wonder… I do remember that George gave Fred credit for helping him make the transition to circuit racing but we the unwashed didn't have much respect. From about day two George F was always much quicker than Fred and we thought for a second driver we could have done better. It didn't help that Howard and wife, Christine, were besties with Fred and his Christine.

Another photo shows the Japanese built car (#56) on a trailer behind our all-white 3-litre E23 Urvan (refer the

Thommo setting the pace up the Newell Hwy in 1981.

chapter on our service vans) on the Newell Highway heading to Bathurst. Also in that photo is a Hertz rent-a-truck leaning into the left turn at Grong Grong. This tyre truck was being driven by Dave Thompson (see 1979 Southern Cross Rally preparation) and the Urvan by Chris Brown, 1981 ARC contender and long-time Datsun/Nissan team helper. The pic was taken by brother/navigator, Simon Brown from the similar, second rig which was trailering Car #55. Bringing up the rear in the convoy was Les Collins driving another E20 van.

Our first Australian-built Bluebird at Braeside

JAMES HARDIE 1000

That first Bathurst 1000 is rather a blur in my mind and I'm not sure if my few memories of those early racing days belong to '81 or '82 but, from the record, in 1981 we qualified pretty well from a class perspective but the race was something of an 'oh well, next year will be better', with George and Fred Gibson, Car #55, dropping out with suspension failure after just 30 of the 120 laps completed by the winner (Dick Johnson), and the Masahiro Hasemi/Kazuyoshi Hoshino, Car #56, retiring with a broken gearbox after 66 laps.

It was a troubled race with lots of carnage and was ended prematurely and dramatically on lap 121 with a huge pile up at McPhillamy Park on top of the mountain. Christine Gibson and Bob Morris came together, blocking the track and several other cars ploughed into them. More than 60 per cent of the race had been completed so it was declared done with Dick Johnson, leader at the end of lap 120, the winner. At least our Bluebirds survived the race bodily unscathed and we'd learned a lot.

Hoshino/Hoshino 31st on the Bathurst grid for 1981

This story continues in my companion book, Nissan Sport: Touring Car Racing in Australia, so for now, back to the 1981 ARC story.

The Alpine Rally in Victoria, held November 21-22 and the final round of the championship for 1981, once again attracted an oversubscribed, sell-out entry despite the already decided Championship. The LCCA (Light Car Club of Australia) organised an exceptional event that was graced with fine and sunny weather. The maximum 80 cars were flagged away at the Bright Speedway and on into the magnificent surrounding pine plantations during a beautiful Saturday morning.

As the last ever event for the Datsun Rally Team, Nissan entered all three remaining Stanzas, George's Australian-built car (having now been repaired since its Amaroo crash and still sporting its twin cam motor) and running as Car #1, the 1980 Dunkerton Cross-winning car, albeit with L20B engine, for Portman and Runnalls running as Car #2, and Fury's Motogard car running as Car #3, allowing Dunkerton and Beaumont a swan-song to their Datsun career together – such magnanimity from team boss Marsden.

The Ovens Valley was Portman's work environment, he having been a forester in the area for some years. At Wodonga, at the end of the second division, he led Fury followed by Dunkerton. In the third

3, 2, 1, Go! Portman blasts away from control in The Alpine.

division Fury got into stride and bettered Portman on most stages, and then threw away his good work by having an off on a bitumen stage (how embarrassing for a budding race driver) and dropping a maximum penalty in the process of recovering. This left Portman in charge with seven minutes up on Slater (Corolla) with Dunkerton a further two minutes back at the Bright over-night stop.

On Sunday morning, back in the pines, Dunkerton's engine blew out a section of its sump gasket and try as we might to stem the blood loss with good ol' ThreeBond, we were not able to get it sealed and Ross had to retire when the oil light came on.

With Geoff once again in cruise mode, the event wound down leaving he and Ross Runnalls winners on 5:58:12, just over nine minutes to the good of Fury/Suffern on 6:07:14 who were nearly seven minutes ahead of a third Stanza, that of Doug Thompson/Ron Lugg.

So ended that golden period of rallying in Australia. We were the last of the major manufacturers in Australia to withdraw

Inglorious end. Dunkerton pushed into the shade at end '81

from the sport and together with the demise of The Castrol International Rally and The Southern Cross International Rally, it seemed like a line had been drawn – definitely an appropriate time for a team, still with fire in the belly, to move on.

So the story continues in *Nissan Sport: Touring Car Racing in Australia*

The CARS

180B (610) SSS

Three works 180B SSSs came to Australia and competed at the top level between 1972 and 1974, two red cars and a lime green one. There was also a blue car that was built in Australia with the assistance of Datsun Rally Team boss, Bruce Wilkinson. It was driven initially by Gil Davis and then by George Fury.

KP610 No.1. For the 1972 Southern Cross Rally a red RHD car, plated TKS55 TA 5002 came out from the works for Edgar Herrmann/Mike Mitchell as Car #2. It placed fourth in that event. John Roxburgh and Mike Mitchell used it for the Dulux Rally in November that year and placed ninth. This car was also run in the 1973 Southern Cross for Murray/Eckert but did not finish. It was later seen in various South Australian state events but I've found no records.

KP610 No.2. Also for the '72 Cross a second red RHD car plated TKS55 TA 5003 and configured with ECGI electronic injection and engine management, arrived for Bruce Wilkinson/Roger Bonhomme. It carried #8 for the event. The ECGI system proved unreliable and made the car hard to drive. It failed to finish the event but stayed on in Australia until at least early 1974. It went on to win the 1973 Alpine Rally crewed by Frank Kilfoyle/Mike Osborne and in 1974 was used by Gil Davis and Frank Kilfoyle for various Victorian events and by George Fury for the Bega Rally as Car #6.

KP610 No.3. For the 1973 Southern Cross Rally an uncharacteristically lime green RHD SOHC Group 2 car plated TKS56 SE 3240 came out for Kilfoyle/Osborne. Running as Car #8, Kilf achieved 6th place with this car in 'the wet one'. In 1974, Bob Watson/Jeff Beaumont used it for the first four rounds of the Victorian Championship, and Fury/Suffern for at least one later round. It was then repainted (on the outside) red white and blue and became Car #18, the Fury/Suffern Southern Cross car in '74. They placed fourth outright and won Group G.

For the 1975 Don Capasco Rally in Canberra (later rebadged as the Castrol International Rally) Peter Wherret/John Bryson used this car to make an episode of Wherrett's popular TV program, 'Torque'. It had a widened white slash on the side to accommodate this name in suitably large letters. Car #40 managed 10th place.

Immediately following The Don Capasco was the '75 Akademos and Frank Kilfoyle/Geoff Boyd ran as Car #12. They led for almost the whole event but hit a tree rather heavily with just a couple of kms to go, irreparably damaging the body.

It was taken to Canberra and reshelled, becoming the famous and very successful yellow 108B SSS campaigned by Greg Carr for Gerry Ball Tuning in 1975-76, winning both the '75 Alpine and the '76 Castrol.

The car's original bodily remains finished life at Sims Metal in Canberra. The story goes that, at first, customs did not approve the crushing as navigational gear and mag wheels were not present. Gerry apparently raced back to the workshop and grabbed a Halda and some wheels, threw them into the doomed car, and bore witness to its demise.

KP610 No.4. A fourth 180B SSS which ran as a semi-works car was a locally sourced, blue-coloured 610 SSS with the 1973 Australian facelift lights and grille treatment. It was intended for Gil Davis/Monty Suffern in the 1973 Southern Cross. Unfortunately (from one perspective) Gil had to withdraw not long into the preparation, so Monty suggested George Fury would make a good replacement. George took over preparation and had it on the start line as Car #35. Although failing to finish a very tough and wet rally (withdrawing in Div. 3) the event proved a good shakedown for car and crew and it went on to place a strong 5th as Car #8 in the 1974 Don Capasco and also ran in the Penfolds Rally that year. The car was sold to John Armitage later that year and many of its components went into John's own 180B SSS.

240Z HS30

Four works 240Zs came to Australia and, with the exception of the LHD car made famous by Ross Dunkerton in 1976 (which turned out to be the reincarnation of Tony Fall's '73 Cross car), none of them stayed here for long.

240Z No.1. 1972 Southern Cross red RHD with plate no. TKS33 SA 8075 for Rauno Aaltonen/Steve Halloran as Car #1. Placed 2nd in the Cross to Andrew Cowan in a Mitsubishi Galant but could conceivably have won if not for a navigational error by Halloran. Subsequently used by Edgar Herrmann/Roger Bonhomme in the '72 Dulux Rally as Car #3, by Kilfoyle/Osborne in the '73 Experts Trial, and then by Bill Evans/Mike Mitchell as Car #9 in the '73 Repco Alpine Rally. It was then not seen again and likely repatriated to Japan.

240Z No.2a. 1973 Southern Cross red LHD with plate no. TKS33 SU 4080 for Tony Fall/Steve Halloran as Car #1. It was rolled and DNF'd and returned home in disgrace.

240Z No.3. 1973 Southern Cross red RHD with plate no. TKS33 SU 3444 for Shehkar Mehta/Roger Bonhomme as Car #2. It suffered rear end damage and DNF'd. It also returned to Japan.

240Z No.4. 1973 Southern Cross. Red LHD with unknown plate no. for Bob Watson/Jeff Beaumont as Car #18. It placed eighth and then presumably returned to Japan as not seen here again.

240Z No.2b. Tony Fall's 1973 red LHD 240Z plate no. TKS33 SU 4080 returned from the presumed dead, looking shiny and straight, for

Ross Dunkerton/Jeff Beaumont to run in the 1975 Southern Cross and for the 1976 ARC season. Sasamoto san, Nissan Australia Vice President made enquiries on Ross' behalf at the rally works at Oppama, trying to secure a car for his use after it became apparent that all cars scheduled for Australia that year were accounted for (Aaltonen, Källström and Fury). All that was available was the LHD 240Z Tony Fall had rolled in the 1973 Cross and which had been repaired. It was duly sent and handed over to team Dunkerton to prepare and support for the '75 Cross as Car #12.

Sadly Ross had a coming together with a spectator's car on a transport section during the first division of the Cross, and damage to the right hand rear suspension arm, and the lack of a replacement, caused his retirement. For the 1976 ARC season the car was brought to the newly set up Australian Datsun Rally Team workshop at Sturt Street, South Melbourne where it was prepared and fully supported from, that year.

Results were: Third, Castrol International as Car #9, First, ARC Vic Marchal Rally as Car #9, First, ARC NSW Bega Valley Rally as Car #2, First, Rally Renault ARC SA as Car #2, First, ARC Vic North Eastern Rally as Car #2, Second, ARC Qld Lutwyche Village Rally as Car #1. Dunkerton and Beaumont were ARC Champion driver and navigator for 1976 with daylight second. Better than gathering dust in Opama, I'm sure you'll agree.

Sadly the ageing Z was starting to break up – cracks developing around suspension mounts etc. and Ross decided it would be less expensive and easier to put all the good stuff from this car into his own 260Z to use for 1977. It was used for the 1977 Castrol International, the ARC Vic North Eastern Rally, won the ARC WA Rally of the West, and then suffered an engine failure due to lost sump plug in the ARC Qld Lutwyche Village Rally.

The 240Zs sounded incredible in the forests at night and even better from the driver's seat in Ross' LHD car, behind those triple, twin throat Solex (Mikuni) carburettors! It had buckets of torque but would rev just as hard as a 4-cyl L-series SOHC of the day. A thrill to drive even though I only did so on the way home from a few events.

Works 240Z in 260Z body for 1977

710 (VIOLET) SSS

I've been able to identify 12 different Japanese works prepared Violet 710s that came to Australia. Difficulties with identification have been caused by the Japanese updating chassis numbers on two Carnet documents meaning that cars arrived in Australia carrying the same Carnet plate as cars that had arrived in previous years, e.g.

1. TKS56 MA 7359 was on Fury's 1975 Cross car and also on Källström's apparently new car for '77.

2. TKS56 MA 7361 was on Aaltonen's 1975 Cross car and also on Makinen's, also brand new looking car, for the '77 Cross.

3. As a variation on the theme, TKS56 RA 5237 was the Carnet plate on Walfridsson's 710 in the 1976 Southern Cross. It was quite heavily damaged from a rollover and side-swiping a tree and, though it finished the event in sixth place, was returned to Japan. TKS56 RA 5237 returned to Australia on the new-looking 710 that Aaltonen/Beaumont drove to our first Cross victory in the 1977 event – it turns out that Walfridsson's car had been repaired and it's only taken me 43 years to learn it was that same car which returned for Aaltonen in 1977. Leftovers often turn out to be better than fresh-cooked meals. This famous plate now sometimes also graces Neil Taylor's immaculate 710.

All 710s were RHD and most were configured for Group 4 or Group G (in Australia) competition with DOHC LZ18 engines, there were four instances though of 710s running in Group 2 spec. with SOHC LR18 (FIA) engines. Mystery surrounds the fate of some of these cars and the burial ground or country exit point of at least two remains unknown.

The known history of cars 1 to 12 is as follows:

710 #01 arrived for the 1974 Southern Cross Rally, blue sided Group 2 car for Källström/Bonhomme, plated TKS56 NI 8640. It DNF'd the Cross with suspension failure after he went off in the first stage of the second Div. Fury/Suffern used it to win the RACV 500 Rally after the Cross and it remained in Australia for at least 1975 during which Fury won the ANZ Bank Mazda House Rally in NSW with Roger Bonhomme (one of the very rare events he did without Monty pointing the way), and also ran the Forrest Classic Rally this time with Monty, but for an unknown result. It did no further events but was used as a service area reconnoitre vehicle for the 1977 Southern Cross.

George with Roger in the 1975 Mazda House Rally

710 #02. Also for the 1974 Southern Cross Rally, a blue sided Group 2 car for Frank Kilfoyle/Ian Richards, plated TKS56 NI 8352. Kilf crashed out of the event early in Div 1 and the car was either crushed or returned to Japan after its return to Melbourne.

710 #03. The 1975 test/development car, blue sided, DOHC and initially with ECGI injection/engine management, plated TKS56 HA 7715. The ECGI was removed at Wilkinson Motors not long after its arrival (probably as soon as Bruce discovered it hadn't been improved much since his unpleasant experience with it on the 180B SSS in the 1972 Cross).

Fury used this car with Monty to come 3rd in the 1975 Akademos Rally and then with Rex Muldoon to zero the Experts Rally, both in VIC.

It then, after the Mid Eastern Rally, running Car Zero as a shakedown, became the Fury/Suffern Car #8 in the 1976 Southern Cross in Group 4 spec. and was leading the event well until midway through the last division when its differential failed and left them forlorn and far from home.

Immediately after the Cross, Shekhar Mehta and Adrian Mortimer used it as Car #2 to place third in the Holden Dealers International in Gippsland, Victoria.

Then, in 1977, resplendent in its new Australian livery (white over blue and with a thin red waistline just above the blue), Fury/Suffern ran it in the Bega Rally as Car #7, Round 4 of ARC, placing second. In September they used it to win the Endrust Rally, running as Car #10.

It was then lent to Gerry Ball Tuning to prepare and run for Dunkerton and Graeme Pilgrim for the 1977 Southern Cross. The poor old girl had apparently had enough though and she DNF'd due to sheared wheel studs and a lost rear wheel during a competitive section in Div. 3 while placed 10th. I've not been able to discover the car's fate – rally cars going to Canberra had a way of disappearing ☹

710 #04. The 1975 Southern Cross was the first event for the new, white-sided livery on the 710s (see Richard Power's dissertation on this new design scheme on page 66). It wasn't to be a lucky colour scheme for the '75 Southern Cross and all three suffered early and catastrophic engine failures – mind you, good luck wasn't easy to come by for us in this era of the Southern Cross Rally.

Initial testing with Fury's new 1975 710.

In September, three new Group 4 spec'd, DOHC-engined cars arrived. The first, plated TKS56 MA 7359, was to be Car #7 for Fury/Suffern.

They led the event into Day 2 and were storming away with a dust-free advantage when a failed big-end bolt created havoc inside the crankcase and it was all over. The same calamity had already befallen Källström and then Aaltonen in the sister cars.

Soon after the 'Cross, George and Monty ran it as Car #1 in the Holden Dealers 500 in Gippsland, coming second to Bond's L34 Torana.

In 1976 Fury began the year well winning the Overture Rally in Victoria with Peter Davis in the left hand seat.

Next up George and Monty scored a good second to Greg Carr in the Castrol International and then won three of the ARC rounds: the Marchal Rally (Vic), the North Eastern Rally (Vic) and the Warana Rally (Qld). A blown head gasket at the Bega Rally (NSW) spoiled the possibility of four consecutive outright wins but with the crazy ARC regulations that year, the car was not eligible for points anyway.

This car's fate is unsure but it was probably later crushed in Melbourne.

710 #05. The second of the new, white-sided, DOHC 710s for 1975 was for Rauno Aaltonen/John Souminen, Car #2, in the Southern Cross with carnet plate TKS56 MA 7361. It suffered the same fate in the Cross as its two sisters, retiring early in Div 2 with catastrophic engine failure.

The car's next event was as Car #2 in the 1976 Castrol International for Peter Wherrett and Alan Cummine. It finished mid-field after a rather tentative drive.

710s #4 and #5 in the same shot – lucky me

Following on from the Castrol it was lent to the Gerry Ball team and became the Carr/Gregson, Car #10, for the '76 Southern Cross where they disappeared off a cliff on the first night and DNF'd. They did far better, however, to win the immediately following '76 Holden Dealers International as Car #6 and then also the Kleber Alpine as Car #4.

Somewhat disconcertingly it appears to have been returned to Melbourne where I find it in photos at Braeside being used as a development rig. (See the story about the development of the deDion rear end for the 710.) The discarded body was later crushed in Melbourne.

710 #06. The third new, white-sided, DOHC 710 for 1975 was for Harry Källström with Roger Bonhomme, running as Car #3 in the Southern Cross and was plated TKS56 MA 7360. It too suffered catastrophic engine failure and withdrew early in Div 2. This failure caused a viewing port to be opened in the side of the engine block making the cause of its demise plain for all to see. I think it was repatriated to Japan and then returned in 1976.

Twelve months later it was Car #4 in the 1976 Southern Cross for Shekhar Mehta with Adrian Mortimer running in Group 2 spec. It placed third, first home for Datsun that year, and was immediately sent to New Caledonia where Jean Ragnotti campaigned it successfully.

710 #07. Three pristine-looking DOHC 710s arrived (to join two remaining from '75) for the 1976 Southern Cross – all three sporting the now international, but Australian conceived, white-sided livery. The first, plated TKS56 ME 6431, had I believe, been Källström's in that

Flame out – sheesh, can't catch a break

year's East African Safari! But was to be Car #7 for Rauno Aaltonen/Jeff Beaumont.

Before heading north though, as a shakedown and before it had any sign-writing or decals, Rauno and Jeff ran it in the Mid Eastern Trial in Victoria as car zero, blitzing the opposition.

Soon after, in the 'Cross though, not even Car #7 could provide luck and they retired with head gasket failure late in Div. 1, following an impact with a bank which caused the engine to move forward and hole the radiator. This car apparently returned to Japan and was repaired and prepared for Aaltonen to use in the following year's East African Safari.

710 #08. The second new arrival for '76 was for Harry Källström/Roger Bonhomme as Car #3 for the Southern Cross and plated TKS56 RA 5226. Its LZ18 twin cam engine failed mid way through the fourth and final division. Harry had been matching times with the leaders and was placed fourth when they stopped.

George and Monty used this car as #4 in the 1976 Holden Dealers International Rally in SE Victoria and placed second.

In the following year they ran it in the North Eastern Rally (Vic ARC) where a rear-end failure caused a DNF.

Then, running as Car #2 in the 1977 Castrol International, George battled hard with Greg Carr, eventually placing second.

Fury/Suffern then also placed second, this time to Dunkerton's 260Z, in the '77 Rally of the West.

The Lutwyche Rally in Qld was the next round. Here George and Monty had a DNF due to a failed distributer drive. Then next it became the Dunkerton/Beaumont Car #3 for the Bega Rally but DNF'd again with engine failure after impaling the radiator on a branch.

In the final ARC round for 1977, the Endrust Rally in SA, Ross and Jeff ran it as Car #8 and this time placed second where this 710 seemed most comfortable – when it could finish.

Very soon afterward it went to Canberra, where it was repainted in the new Total Oil Australia colours.

Maybe old but it could still fly. Ross in NC.

Gerry Ball Tuning prepared it for Bob Watson/Peter Godden to run as Car #12 in the 1977 Southern Cross. It placed third and completed a trifecta for Datsun. From here it went off to New Caledonia for Dunkerton/Beaumont to use as Car #3 in the 1977 NC Safari, and finally had a win. It did not return.

710 #09. The third 710 that arrived for the 1976 Cross was for Per Inge Walfridsson/Peter Godden as Car #16 and carried the plate TKS56 RA 5237. The exciting Walfridsson managed a rollover on Div. 1 and to side-swipe a tree in Div. 3. But he was quick enough, always there or there abouts, and he persisted – in the end rewarded by a good sixth place.

Man on a mission, out of the way dog. Oops

After returning to Japan the car was repaired and was reincarnated as the Aaltonen/Beaumont Car #3 for the '77 Southern Cross. Apart from striking a dog during the transport section north up the Pacific Highway at the beginning of Div 4, they were quick, had a consistent run, and won the event! Ecstatically, Nissan had won a Southern Cross Rally at last and, with Källström/Billstam placing second and Watson/Godden third, scored a trifecta after struggling for several years to even get on the podium. The winning car was immediately shipped back to Nissan's hall of glory in its museum at Zama, Japan where it remains (photo on page 159 shows the car as it remains today at Zama).

710 #10. For 1977, four apparently brand new 710s arrived. This one would be Car #1 for World Rally Championship aces, Timo Makinen/Henry Liddon. It carried plate TKS56 MA 7361, same as Aaltonen's 1975 Cross car (710 No.6 above) initially creating some confusion as to whether it really was a new car, but as Aaltonen's '75 Cross car was still in Australia carrying that plate, it must have been.

Timo Makinen/Henry Liddon, this time in a Datsun

It suffered a light rollover during Div. 3, and then somehow managed to hole its cast aluminium dry sump during the final division and, with no oil, retired after most of a hard-fought event and with the end in sight.

This car was one of two repainted in the TOTAL DATSUN livery at the start of 1978. There was however, insufficient time to complete this before the cars were shipped to WA for the first event and both cars competed there in white and blue without the red stripe and had TOTAL DATSUN signage stuck on rather than painted.

George with John Large in 710 #10. Shakedown for '78 Rally of the West

On the weekend before the ARC event, George did a state championship round, the Experts Cup, there with John Large navigating. Crews then flew home and returned a week later with Monty to do the first ARC round of the Australian Championship running as Car #2. This 710 placed second to Dunkerton/Beaumont's sister car.

It then went on to do the Lutwyche Rally in Qld as Car #1, where it suffered brake problems and a broken shocker, not finishing in the placings. Then the Donlee Rally (NSW round) where George and Monty finished the car's career with a win as Car #5. We'd been led to expect kangaroos!

This 710 was finally stripped of its best bits at Braeside and those replaced with standard parts before it

Fury's Donlee 710. A good win to finish up

was crushed in Melbourne. With Howard's blessing many of its good bits were pressed back into service in Chris and Simon Brown's 180B SSS rally car.

710 #11. The second new 710 for the '77 Cross was for Harry Källström/Claes Billstam as Car #4. It carried Carnet plate TKS56 MA 7359 (again the same plate number as a '75 Cross car, this time Fury's). They finished second to Rauno/Jeff Beaumont.

This car became the Dunkerton/Beaumont 1978 ARC car, painted in the TOTAL DATSUN Australian colour scheme described above. After also doing the one week earlier WA state round (Fury and Dunkerton were likely running Car 0 and 00), Dunko and Beauy as Car #1 were able to win the main event, Round 1 of the ARC, the Rally of the West.

They placed second in the Lutwyche in Qld (Car #3), suffered an engine failure while leading Fury in the Donlee in NSW as Car #6, placed second to Carr's RS1800 Escort at Bega, NSW as Car #5, and DNF'd with water in the fuel at the Endrust Rally in SA running as Car #7. This 710 too was stripped at Braeside and crushed at Sims Metal.

710 #12. The third new 710 for 1977 was for Fury/Suffern. It carried plate TKS56 HA 7717 and was Car #6 for the Southern Cross that year. George struggled with its handling all event (I think wishing he'd been able to use the 710 he'd sorted to his liking and had just used to win the SA Round of the ARC a month or two earlier – 710 #03 above. Unfortunately it no longer had the international livery preferred by Nissan's marketing people for the big international event.). George had managed to stay reasonably competitive, though, probably by driving near his limit. Within sight of the finish of this long and gruelling Southern Cross and running third at the time, most of the way back to Kempsey from Bellingen, and just changing into fifth gear on a very fast, cresty road, they came unstuck at a tricky right hand kink. The car flipped and rolled multiple times, ending up quite a way from where the incident began.

The dead 710 yard out the back of the Total Service Station at Port Macquarie.

The remains, after it left the dead 710 lot behind the Total service station in Port Macquarie, sat in the dead car lot behind our workshop at Braeside for some time, before being crushed at Simms Metal.

...and the other side. Yep, definitely a write off.

PA10/11 STANZA

I've been able to identify eight PA10/11 (LHD/RHD) Stanza cars that originated from Oppama, Japan as 'works' rally cars, plus one which we built in Australia and used alongside the Japanese-built Stanzas.

Stanza #01. Our first Stanza arrived mid 1978 to begin Australian development and shake-down for the '78 Southern Cross Rally. It carried Carnet plate TKS57 NI 445. Its first event was the Goldfields Rally (a VIC championship event entered for testing) where the drum brakes, fitted to its live rear axle, were identified as a shortcoming. The 710s had always been fitted with disc brakes on their independent rear.

The car then received a full respray in Australian TOTAL DATSUN livery in time for the Bega Rally, fourth round of the ARC in '78. George ran as Car #6 and we discovered that the aluminium diff centre housing was not up to the job and its failure gave us our first Stanza DNF.

The car's second major event was ARC round 5, the Endrust Rally in South Australia where George was Car #10. He became badly bogged and finished mid-field.

This car only did one more event, the 1978 Southern Cross Int'l Rally as Car #6 running under international Group 5 and with a world-first LZ20B engine that I built. It won! After an inauspicious start, its short career ended in glory and it was immediately shipped back to Japan, via the Geneva Motor Show, and remains in the Nissan Museum at Zama to this day.

Cross winning Stanza on display at the Geneva Motor Show on way back to Japan

Stanza #02. Our second PA11 carried Carnet plate no. TKS57 TE 8013 and arrived as one of three new Stanzas for the 1978 Southern Cross, this one in Group 2 SOHC spec. for Ross Dunkerton and Adrian Mortimer running as Car #5. It had a pretty good 'Cross, Ross with the bit between his teeth determined to show the lower powered car wasn't going to be a handicap, and they placed fourth O/R and first in Group 2 class.

A steady run to 4th O/R and 1st in Group 2 in the 1978 Southern Cross Rally.

After the Cross, in the Marchal Rally in Victoria (final round of the ARC) and now in the Australian TOTAL DATSUN livery (tapering horizontal red stripe above blue at bottom) and with a DOHC engine, Ross and Jeff Beaumont, running as Car #3, brought the Stanza home in a fine second place to Greg Carr's Ford Escort.

For the 1979 ARC season Ross and Jeff mostly used this car to win Ross' 4th Australian Rally Drivers Championship (Jeff's 3rd), placing second in the Akademos in Victoria as Car #6, third in W.A.'s Rally of the West as Car #4, first in the Lutwyche in Queensland as Car #2, and third after a big rollover, in the Bega in NSW as Car #6.

A sad looking Stanza in its last event in Oz

They used Stanza #04 to sew up the title with third place in the final ARC round, the Endrust, that year. At the end of 1979 Stanza #02 was crushed due to extensive damage from the Bega rollover.

Stanza #03. The third new PA11 from Japan in 1978 was an LZ18-engined, Group 5 car for Rauno Aaltonen and Jeff Beaumont, carrying Carnet plate TKS57 TE 8010.

After starting in the '78 Endrust as a shake-down for the 'Cross it broke a camshaft timing gear before the first competitive.

It then ran as Car #1 in the '78 Cross but both Japanese LZ18 powered Stanzas suffered catastrophic engine failure in the Cross that year and this was to continue an unfortunate pattern for this particular car.

After the Cross, Stanza #03 was given the new Australian TOTAL DATSUN livery and George/Monty used it for the 1978 Marchal Rally,

Victorian ARC round #6, that followed soon after the Cross. Tom Snooks' account would have me believe it again suffered a broken camshaft drive gear but I'm rather suspicious. I think this had become Howard's 'go to' cause of DNF.

Fury & Suffern 2nd at Bega in '79. One of just two successes for this Stanza.

For the 1979 ARC season, Fury and Suffern began well by winning the Akademos Rally in VIC but then suffered three DNFs firstly in the Rally of the West in WA, then the Castrol International in ACT (both engine-related) and then another in the Lutwyche Rally in QLD, this time attributable to the driver. The Bega Valley Rally in NSW produced a more promising second place (to Colin Bond) but then a heavy crash in the Endrust, SA, saw a DNF in the car's swan-song event. Not really a happy car and the body subsequently crushed in Melbourne.

Stanza #04. The fourth new PA11 for '78 was a Group 5 DOHC powered car for Harry Källström and Claes Billstam. This car carried Carnet plate TKS57 RU 7691. Harry and Claes too had a disappointing Southern Cross, withdrawing with engine failure.

Dunkerton and Beaumont came third in the '79 Endrust Rally in SA with this car as part of their championship winning year.

A little later that year, somewhat interestingly, this Stanza was used by Rex Muldoon to make a film of a trip to Alice Springs. It turned out rather cringeworthy and he went back to his day job.

Shoulda, coulda, woulda in PNG 1980

It sat around as a spare car, then in late 1980 Ross managed to get have shipped to Papua New Guinea for the 3-day PNG Independence Rally and I was invited along to navigate. We were leading by a mile until I made a gaffe on the last night and a pissed-off Ross drove the last spectator special stage on the final morning with all the valves bouncing until one dropped into its cylinder. Sad.

I believe this car remained in Port Moresby and was later used in local rallies under the Boroko Motors banner .

In 1979 one PA10 and one PA11 that had been used in the Motogard Rally in New Zealand were subsequently brought to Australia to be two of the three '79 Southern Cross Stanzas. Both had been run in NZ as Group 2 SOHC cars but were converted to Group 5 DOHC spec. soon after arrival here.

Stanza #05 had been Andy Dawson's in NZ and was a RHD body. For the 'Cross it was the Fury/Suffern Car #6 and carried Australian rego no. YJT 525 (Datsun rally cars were, for the first time, registered here in the Australian Capital Territory). George and Monty brought it home in first place to claim their second successive Southern Cross Rally win.

Pre-loved Datsuns seemed to do better in Oz

There'd been a bit of rego plate shuffling and this car from now carried YJT 515 – pinched from #07 below, which had just left for Nouméa.

George and Monty's 1979 Stanza 'office'.

In the 1980 ARC, Portman/Runnalls placed fourth in the Bega with it, then won the Donlee round. And finally Portman and Phil Rainer won the 1980 Martini Mountain Rally in S.A. with it, all still in Japanese works livery.

It was 'sold' to Midway Motors for Ron Cremen's use at end 1980 and was later on-sold several times and re-bodied before going to the U.K. and Portugal and, at last report, back in Japan, albeit in private hands.

Stanza #06. Dunkerton's 1979 Southern Cross car was a new PA11 from Oppama in Group 5 configuration with an LZ DOHC engine and registered in Australia as YJT 505. For the '79 Cross it ran as Car #4 and Dunkerton/Beaumont brought it home in second place. It would go on to end up with the best record for any of our Stanzas.

On its way to becoming the last SCR winner

For 1980 it was re-painted in the new TOTAL DATSUN livery and Ross and Jeff used it for the Australian Championship, picking up an engine related DNF in the Rally of the West, third in the Lutwyche, first in the Akademos, third at Bega, and another engine related DNF in the Donlee – enough for third place in the ARC that year.

The car was then updated with the rectangular headlights and new tail lamps etc. for Ross and Jeff to run in the 1980 Southern Cross as Car #4. They won the event by just three minutes from great rival, Greg Carr in his works BDG Escort, Ross was finally able to put a Southern Cross Rally winner's trophy in the cabinet.

For 1981, as we no longer had Ford Escorts to beat, I'd built a modified L20B single cam motor for Stanza #06, so with that fitted and updated again with a new DATSUN paint scheme, mostly white and black, #06 became the Portman/Runnalls 1981 ARC dominating Stanza. Four consecutive first places: the Lutwyche, Bega, Akademos and Alpine Rallies.

#06 Stanza finishing in a blaze of glory

Geoff also won the Woodley Wines 500 SARC Rnd 4 with Phil Rainer.

This Stanza was 'sold' (no $s ever changed hands) to, and campaigned by, Phil Horan in South Australia.

Subsequently it was mysteriously moved to a shed in Darwin, spending many years there rusting away. It is now undergoing a thorough restoration (body work in the hands of Laurie Wilson) by Graham Symons in country Victoria.

Stanza #07. The third car for the 1979 Southern Cross was the second of the two from New Zealand, a Group 2, LHD PA10 driven in the Motogard to second place and a Group 2 victory by Timo Salonen (but subsequently disqualified at scrutineering). It was registered in the ACT as YJT 515 and run by Aaltonen and Mortimer as Car #2 in the Southern Cross and completing Nissan's trifecta by placing third after Fury and Dunkerton.

Rauno & Mort head out of PMac in the LHD PA10

The car was shipped to New Caledonia after the Cross for Ross and Jeff to run the New Caledonia Safari. They had a huge crash in the event and the Stanza was written off. It died in Japanese works livery.

Late news is that it has risen from the dead and now resides in the Philippe Pentacost collection in Noumea.

Stanza #08. For the 1980 Australian Championship we built a new Stanza from a brand new body shell. It was light and strong, had a 2140cc LZ engine and incorporated all we'd learned along the way. It was initially painted in the 1980 Australian livery (see bottom page 170) and was given George's YJT 525 rego.

In the 1980 ARC, Fury/Suffern won three of the five events, Rally of the West, Lutwyche Rally, Bega Valley Rally, suffering an engine related DNF in the Akademos Rally and placing third in the Donlee Rally – they had a dominant win in the championship.

The 1980 Southern Cross though, was a disaster with loss of oil pressure and failed engine – again while leading the event in the last division and within sight of the end. I don't remember the details – I must have blocked it out ☹

The result of the year-ending Alpine Rally was nearly as disappointing: fourth place behind Carr's Ford Escort, Portman's Datsun 1600, and Bond's Escort

For 1981 Stanza #08 was updated with the new tail lamps etc. and repainted in the same scheme as the Stanza SSS that was being sold to the public in an attempt to portray the rally car as 'off the showroom floor'. George and Monty began their year with a very memorable win in the Castrol International Rally in ACT during which we swapped in much lower and firmer suspension and wider slick tyres for the first division, in daylight, on tarmac.

They followed up with a third in the Datsun trifecta at the Lutwyche ARC round in Queensland.

Fury's sights though were now on Nissan's planned circuit racing and this car was used as George's 'training' car for what was to come. Unfortunately though, it was damaged in an accident at Amaroo and George had to sit out

The very adaptable, Oz-made Stanza at Sandown

the Bega Valley Rally and use Ross' car for the Akademos Rally while #08 was being repaired between late May and November in 1981, so busy were we with other things.

The final event, and success, with this car was in the Alpine Rally that year where George and Monty placed second to Portman.

It was finally 'sold' to Bob Nicoli in Western Australia who promptly wrote it off, breaking its back on a huge rock. Also very sad.

Stanza #09. Following the 1980 Motogard Rally in NZ, where George and Monty placed a creditable fourth in an international field, this Stanza was sent over the Tasman and converted from Group 2 to Group 5 (LZ20 engine, dry sumping, fibreglass panels and, rather strangely, front and rear spoilers) by the Japanese engineers for Portman and Runnalls to use in the 1980 Southern Cross as Car #5. It also came with new model taillights and various body trim.

The carnet plate it carried was KNY59 TA 2955 but, in the Motogard, also had local NZ rego plates – JM5943. In Australia it was locally registered as YMZ 555.

Geoff and Ross leading until this point in Div 3

In the Cross, Portman was very quick, coming second at end of Div.1 and leading after Div.2. He came unstuck in Div.3 though, clipping a log and breaking the front suspension. He rejoined in sixth place and was gaining until his LZ engine failed with yet another broken cam shaft drive gear.

After the Cross Geoff teamed with Phil Rainer (the Australian Martini agent) to run the Martini Mountain Rally. They won convincingly.

For 1981 this became the Dunkerton/Beaumont ARC car. They had a win in Round One in WA, a second to Portman in Queensland, a blown diff and DNF in the Bega, and a DNF with a badly leaking sump gasket in the Alpine.

George with Monty were then given #09 for the Akademos Rally, their own Stanza not yet ready after damage from a Sports Sedan race incident, and achieved second place behind Portman.

As a trade-off for having to miss the Akademos Rally, Dunkerton and Beaumont got to run this car in the Macleay 1000 off-road race, between the Bega and the Akademos Rallies, coming second by only 24 seconds to a serious off-road buggy.

#09 was 'sold' to Peter Philips from Queensland at the end of 1981 and he used it to win his 1982 state championship.

It has had at least five subsequent Australian owners and, in recent times, an extensive and very accurate restoration has been completed by Jeff Cameron in Melbourne.

Tired car and crew at finish of the Macleay 1000

Stanza development in Australia

Peter Davis has provided some detail on the Stanza development in Australia from 1978.

Driveline development

In early to mid-1978 Nissan Japan sent a factory built Rally Stanza to Australia for evaluation and feedback to assist with their upcoming participation in the '78 Cross with this new car.

In many ways the car was a backward step as it was initially fitted with a single cam LR20B engine and rear drum brakes whereas the 710s had been developed with disc brakes all round and a Twin Cam engine, a package that had achieved considerable success throughout the world. The apparent advantage was lighter weight and live rear axle as opposed to the IRS on the 710.

Concurrently the factory was also switching from independent rear end (180B) to live axle for volume production (200B) so there was a synergy. The production Stanza was also live rear end.

The car delivered to Braeside went into its evaluation phase with an inglorious start. During the first testing session at Mt. Slide in the Yarra Valley, Victoria, with Team Manager Howard Marsden in the car, George Fury clipped a stump on the inside of a corner and the car disappeared over the edge, needing to be winched back onto the road a couple of hours later by the team.

The damage was not too severe and was repaired over the next few weeks to enable further testing.

Rally testing was conducted in a local event run by the Renault Car Club and already rear brake issues were becoming apparent as the longevity of the rear brakes was minimal, as was their performance.

Pete and Jamie busy solving brake and diff issues ;-)

The car was entered in the 1978 Bega Valley Rally, a round of the Australian Championship where it became apparent that the differential was also an issue requiring attention if the car was to be reliable. Various rear brake shoe materials were tried including the much-heralded metallic linings, all to no avail and several shoe changes were required throughout the event.

The car was retired with a broken crown wheel and pinion which triggered the decision to redesign the rear driveline and brakes.

Evaluation and resolution of differential problem

The differential failure was thought to be the result of an aluminium centre differential housing being used in place of the standard but heavier, cast iron housing. Aluminium was used to reduce the unspring weight of the rear axle assembly.

It was thought that the housing was distorting under load allowing misalignment which resulted in unusually high loads being placed on the differential gears and causing premature failure.

This issue was easily resolved by replacing the aluminium housing with a readily available cast iron part as used in the small commercial range of Datsun vehicles.

Whilst Japan did not agree with the diagnosis the change was made and no further differential issues were encountered.

Authors note: I am not sure what happened in later years ie. whether the cast iron continued to be used or reverted back to aluminium. The '78 Japanese Cross cars used aluminium housings but the cars did not last long enough due to engine failure to make an evaluation.

The Japanese spare diffs sent out for the Cross are part of another story which will be related later.

Resolution of rear brake problem

The rear brake inadequacy was an issue that had to be resolved if the car were to be reliable and competitive.

Clearly disc brakes were the only option but this presented its own problem with the known phenomenon of brake 'knock off'.

The standard rear drive axle relied on a single row conventional axle bearing for its outer support. Whilst adequate for a drum brake arrangement it was not so for a disc brake arrangement. With the single bearing arrangement the axial movement of the axle within the bearing was transferred to the disc (bolted solidly to the axle) which in turn would transfer this movement to the hydraulic caliper pistons causing them to be partially pushed back into the caliper leaving a gap between the disc pad and disc.

This gap has to be taken up on the next brake application which uses part (or all) of the pedal travel to push the pads back into contact with the disc before any braking force can be applied. Brake pedal 'pumping' is intolerable in a competitive rally car. The knock off is exacerbated by the continual side to side sliding of rally cars. Several slides in each direction may take place before a brake pedal application is required, by which time the gap between the hydraulic pistons and disc can be substantial. The general accepted engineering method was to use a 'full floating axle' whereby the drive hub and disc are solidly mounted on opposing bearings, much the same as a front wheel assembly, and the drive axle being supported at the inner end by splining into the differential side gears and bolting to the drive hub at the outer end. As the hub and disc are solidly supported and cannot move there is no push back of the brake caliper pistons thus a full brake pedal is available for each application.

This option, although used by Colin Bond in the successful 'Sierra' adaptation on his locally prepared Escorts, was not available to the Datsun Rally Team.

As a local solution we searched out a wide double row bearing which I think was to be found in standard bearing catalogues of the time and set about adapting it into the Stanza rear end.

Fortunately the machined section of the Stanza rear axle allowed the fitting of a wider bearing and there was a machined stepped down diameter on the axle which was suitable for a new 'shrink ring' which was made to retain the wider bearing.

Shrink rings are a steel collar with an internal diameter slightly smaller than the machined section of the axle. They were pressed or shrunk on to the axle after the bearing was fitted – the interference fit between the axle and the ring provided sufficient resistance to allow any lateral force on the bearing attempting to dislodge it to be resisted thus holding the bearing in position. It was not uncommon for shrink rings to fail and many punters welded the rings onto the axle so they could not move. This usually had poor results owing to the welding creating stress points in the highly stressed axles thus resulting in axle breakage.

So with that part resolved the issue was how to contain the wider bearing that now protruded beyond the axle housing. This was accomplished by fabricating brake caliper brackets that fitted over the unsupported part of the bearing and bolted to the axle housing. The bracket acted as the bearing retainer plate as well as caliper mount. This in effect widened the outer bearing support area as the new bracket became part of the axle housing and the complete outside of the bearing was now supported. It worked very well other than an issue in the latter stages of the '78 Cross…"

Suspension development

Suspension development continued on from the work done during the later days of the 710's.

George Fury was the 'driver' of the ongoing work and was generally the arbiter of what worked and what didn't.

From the early days the works cars used suspension settings that were too hard. Shocker and strut settings were generally based on force / velocity graphs obtained from a shock absorber dynamometer. The shock absorber or strut would be bolted to the machine and cycled at a particular speed, generally .33 metres/second and .66 metres/second. The resistance of the component being tested would cause the motion of a pencil mounted on a mechanical linkage to create a trace on graph paper mounted on the dyno.

From this we were able to set particular benchmarks to judge the results of any changes that were made – and there were many changes over the years. The graphs and road testing would determine what particular settings might be used for a particular event.

The rear Tokico and KYB gas shockers were difficult to work with and I recall having Tokico shock absorber pistons machined to integrate Bilstein valve components to achieve more precise settings. Up to and including the '78 Cross we used the factory Tokico or KYB units with valving we modified locally. The same was true of the front struts. The 'factory' struts and rear shock absorbers were a spin off from the gruelling East Africa Safari design and they were physically almost unbreakable due to their solid construction, but their on road performance left a lot to be desired.

Interestingly this was the early days of gas shockers and there were fundamental differences between the designs of the Japanese products and the German made Bilstein and De Carbon.

Punters would attempt to compress a Tokico strut or shocker by hand. On a conventional oil shocker the shaft could be compressed into the shocker body with some resistance. Most people thought this resistance was indicative of the 'shocker setting' but that was not really the case as this resistance was only the slow speed resistance and had not much to do with the required settings for a rally car.

If you were to try and compress a Japanese works strut or shocker they would be impossible to move leading the uneducated punter to believe that the shocker settings were extremely hard. What they were in fact experiencing was the result of a high gas pressure reacting on a large shaft and had little to do with the actual settings which were still controlled by oil and valving as in a conventional hydraulic shock absorber. The gas pressure was to provide lift and to prevent the oil foaming under harsh conditions.

25mm extra rear shock travel

Other misconceptions were that Bilstein struts had a larger shaft compared to the Japanese units but this was also incorrect as the Bilstein strut was basically a conventional shock absorber turned upside down and inserted into a strut housing, so that what could be seen was in fact the body of the unit, the small shaft being hidden inside the strut housing. The fact that you could hand compress a Bilstein was because the shaft was of a relatively small diameter and resulted in less area being presented to the gas pressure.

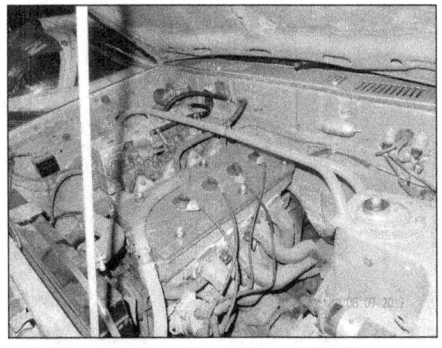

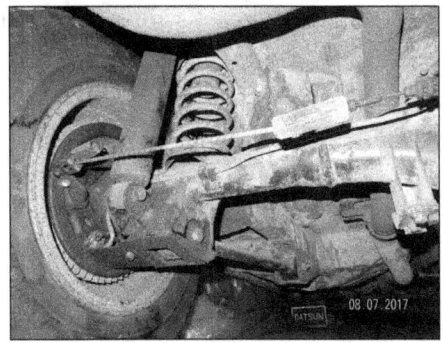

Suspension travel and rear geometry were other areas that were modified on the local car.

The rear end of the cars would hop up and down violently under harsh braking on bitumen. I remember the guys driving flat out on a roadway which ran beside the parts warehouse in Braeside where we worked, testing this phenomenon. The driveway had unmanned access doors into the warehouse and I shudder to think what could have happened if a forklift had suddenly issued forth.

The problem was fixed with the help of the engineers at Nissan's Clayton manufacturing plant. They did lots of drawings and analysis that resulted in the moving of the rear suspension arm mounting points.

The Escorts of the day were often shown in photos with their rear ends squatting and one front wheel in the air when accelerating in corners. I vaguely recall trying to emulate this on the Stanzas and thus having a couple of top arm mount positions which, when adjusted, would give squat or anti squat results.

The rear shocker turrets were extended into the boot area to allow more suspension travel and a panhard rod was also fitted. Not sure what the panhard rod achieved given the standard suspension arms were angled inwards to assist with lateral location but we must have reckoned it worked.

So with Derek doing his bit with the engine we headed off to the Cross, or so we thought... In case you missed it, the rest of this story can be found beginning back on page 105.

The photo above was taken inside the boot of George's '78 Southern Cross winning Stanza in recent years by Graham Symons who was visiting Nissan's Motorsports Heritage Museum in Zama, Japan. He was able to take detailed photos of anything that was of interest to him at the time. Some of these have proven useful in the restoration of his and Jeff Cameron's works Stanzas.

Here too are his photos of the engine bay and the rear axle/suspension. Maybe only I would notice that this isn't the motor that did the Cross – the actual one was most likely swapped out for examination. Any trained eye though, would notice that the rear end shown here has drum brakes so Pete Davis' disc brake rear end had also been swapped out. Both components no doubt became the basis for the development of the Japanese improved versions that appeared in the 1979 cars.

PB210 SUNNY

Along with four new-looking 710s a 1600cc LZ-engined Sunny arrived from Japan for the Southern Cross in 1977. This was to be Car #5 for Shekhar Mehta and Adrian Mortimer.

We Australian crew had almost nothing to do with this car during the event or after as it was serviced by the Japanese and after the Cross went to Gerry Ball Tuning's black hole for several years.

Some stories have emerged regarding its post-Cross history.

Gerry Ball Tuning Chief Mechanic, Lachlan Maclean tells us that... *"The car was driven from Canberra to Melbourne on the Friday before the [Alpine] by one of our 'non mechanical' part time people. It got as far as Tumblong, near Gundagai, before the gearbox fell apart thanks to a bent tailshaft that vibrated the back off the box. Gotta love the 'non mechanical' touch!*

I drove down to Tumblong, pulled the box out and managed to build one from various parts that would get the car to Melbourne. Because of the bent tailshaft, Gerry told us not to go over 80 KPH, which was done, but it added hours to the trip. After a couple of hours sleep in Melbourne, we went to Braeside, replaced the gearbox with a good one, but didn't replace the clutch.

From my recollection, the [Alpine] failure was that the centre of the clutch plate broke, I believe [as] a result of [strain on the clutch plate] during the two gearbox replacements done in the 24 hours before the event. In retrospect, we (I) should have replaced the clutch when I fitted the new gearbox at Nissan in Melbourne the morning before the start. I can't remember why I didn't, but cost was probably one of the reasons.

Regardless, it was a bloody good time to be alive and I have fond memories of this little beast."

Bob Watson's story. "I may have driven that car for Gerry Ball in a local ACT event before driving it in the 1977 Alpine Rally. In the Alpine we [myself and Wayne Gregson] were leading the event after the Escorts of Carr and Bond had problems. With 30 kms to go the centre came out of the [clutch] leaving the car with no drive. To that point we had used 36 tyres. The original plan was for Nissan to leave the car with Gerry Ball and for Nissan to supply a 2 litre DOHC engine for the 1978 season. Howard Marsden reneged on the deal when he suspected our car might be quicker than the factory cars. Gerry got annoyed and hid the car, and the rest is another story."

Following top level Vic/ACT backroom negotiations, in 1982 Geoff Portman drove to Canberra to collect what he expected to be just the 4-valve cylinder head from this car but Ball, who'd apparently decided it was by then surplus to requirements, said, "why don't you take the whole car." The photo shows it just off the trailer in Geoff's back paddock, being admired by a young Nicholas Portman.

The 4-valve (LZ) cylinder head was later adapted to one of Les Collins' large capacity L20B engines and it ran in the Bluebird that Geoff used for various events in the mid 80s.

David Ballard in Canberra is currently engaged in a thorough restoration of this car. I believe it will be powered by an LZ14 twin cam built for it by renowned New Zealand engine man, Reg Cook.

G60 PATOL DESERT RACER

Late in 1976 Howard Marsden got Torqued (sic) into building an off-road vehicle for Peter Wherrett to run in the following year's BP Desert Rally (which was really a race) at Hattah in far north-western Victoria. It may have actually been HM's idea but I couldn't resist the pun.

The G60 patrol, which was by then already old (originally released as it was in 1959) and would definitely have been needing a sales boost, was chosen and Barry Nelson got to work on it right away.

Firstly its weight was reduced by about two thirds by discarding the enormous 4-litre engine, the equally enormous three-speed gearbox and transfer case, and the huge front diff. It was then fitted up with a spare LR18 engine from a 710 and 5-speed, Option 1, non-overdrive gearbox. Suitable shock absorbers were sourced and fitted, along with some snazzy red racing seats, and it was about ready to test.

It was driven in the event by Wherrett and Bill Evans – two legs each. Peter rolled it in his first leg so that one was finished by Bill who then proceeded to give Wherret a driving lesson. They placed 31st out of the 200-odd four-wheeled vehicles. I've no idea what happened to it afterwards.

620 RALLY UTE!

Following the relative success of the hot-rodded G60 Patrol the previous year, for 1978 it was decided to 'do a number' on a 620 Datsun ute for some fun in the dirt. Who knows why, but there were doubtless a few white wines consumed during the deciding.

The job of building this folly was given to Johnny Bosua, a long-time team mechanic from part-time rallying days, who had BGM Motors, an auto repair business in Vermont, Victoria. Once again the motor (4-cyl pushrod) and (4-speed column-shift gearbox) were left on the shop floor and the good old LR18 (with FIA head) and 5-speed, Option1 gearbox were fitted along with vented rally disc brakes for the front, a strengthened disc brake rear end and good Bilstein shockers all round.

It was to be Ross Dunkerton's toy for the 1978 Castrol International but it needed a shake down before hand and Ross and I ran a Victorian special stage event that began in Narbethong in it, with un-remembered results. I do remember it was fun though. The Castrol in 1978 was pretty wet unfortunately and the ute really struggled for traction so even with Dunko driving it wasn't very competitive with the top entries. It broke rear shock mounts in the night division which delayed them and resulted in a mid-field result. I don't know what else it did or what became of it.

Bob Watson was involved too! *"I remember doing some suspension work on the ute, at Howard Marsden's request, at Mount Disappointment. Softened rear springs, fiddled with shockers. Good fun."*

E20 SERVICE VANS

The name Urvan arrived around 1980, in the 70s they were just called E20s. The first one (LYK 653) had already done several rallies as a 4-cyl and was upgraded in a hurry by Barry Nelson in 1976. (Baz had come to us from V8 racing with Allan Moffat in the U.S.A.)

Duncan Hollowood (left) and myself at Braeside loading up to go rallying in '79.

A second hand 240K motor was sourced from Datspares and Baz cut and shut the body to fit it in, chopping out approximately 300mm from the centre of the box section that ran behind the seats!

The gearbox mount was moved back and the column-shift gear selector rods were lengthened by cutting them in half and welding in pieces of angle iron. It was all a bit rough but certainly did the job.

He then used an adaptor to bolt on a 2-barrel Holley carb and made up a very rough (by today's standards) air cleaner, which turned out to be the least reliable part of the van and it was remade several times.

It had a standard exhaust manifold and a 2.5" exhaust with a single straight-through muffler. The rally front hubs went straight onto the E20 stub axles and I can't quite remember how but he adapted the Sumitomo 4-spots onto the uprights. For the rear he just re-drilled the axles and brake drums to suit the 4-stud rally wheels.

That engine lasted until midway through 1978 and then Jamie (it had become his van) got an L28 (from Datspares again, I assume) to replace it. Unfortunately this had implications for a rally result, see story page 100.

The second E20 conversion was done in early 1977 (IKF 895). It was crewed by Barry Nelson and me and then Pete Ryan and myself. It got a second hand 260Z motor (but might have been a 260C) again with an adapted Holley 2-barrel but this time a shorter adaptor was welded to the manifold allowing the carby to be lower. The assembly was ported out to make it all flow much better. The lower carby allowed a better air cleaner to be constructed and it proved very reliable. That engine outlasted the rally team but I remember it was getting tired toward the end.

Both early vans had standard gearboxes initially but some time after, we worked out how to put the standard extension housing (with levers to connect the gear change rods) onto an overdrive 5-speed so they both had 5-speed boxes after that. Both also had driver and navigator Japanese rally seats which added to the sensation of being in a hot-rod. Jamie's van also had a third one of these seats that faced backwards and slotted into a special quick-release bracket. Howard often rode in it!

We had 100 litre rally fuel cells fitted inside over the near-side rear wheel well but before the 1977 Cross, Baz made up a 200 litre all-alloy tank, which stood vertically just inside the rear door on the near side. It had a hose with bowser nozzle on it, the intention to fill the rally cars, as well as supply the van. It didn't go well as the tank split on the second night somewhere north west of Port Macquarie and we ended up having to drain about 100 litres on the side of a gravel road.

It was funny to see the dis-belief on peoples' faces at service stations when we were putting nearly 200 litres in the very high filler neck on the side of the E20.

The third van was an early, brand new E23 Urvan and was originally intended to replace the very tired LYK 653. I built a special engine for it with 3 x 45mm Webers and extractors, big pistons, a big job on the ports, to match the manifolds and the extractors, and a camshaft that I can't remember much about. This one had a 5-speed box from new and with 260Z ratios I think!

This was all happening about the same time as we were ending rallying and beginning circuit racing and I don't think it ever

L30 engine about to be jacked up under the brand new Urvan

went to a rally as we were onto the Bluebird by then. It may have gone to a few rallies in 1981 but was mainly used to trailer race cars to testing/practice sessions and then race meetings before we got our pantech.

Howard later gave it to Wyn (Fred's mechanic) and, to my disappointment, it went off to Sydney. It never even got painted up in war colours. Quite sad really.

Maybe the feature, other than the 6-cyl OHC engine, that made these vans so quick was their standard 5.1:1 diff ratio, although it also helped make them pretty thirsty. It was the same final drive ratio the rally cars used most of the time and they too were impressively quick on the highway – passing at 100kph was so easy. The vans with similar ratios and not much less power (although carrying more weight) were also surprisingly good for passing. With the weight in the back mostly at floor level, the wider, good quality and reasonably soft compound tyres (with most of the blocks removed by the rally cars, together with a lowered body, also meant they felt like they were on rails and you could hammer them through corners.

Another secret weapon was that we often travelled in pairs, 2-way radio connected. That meant that when we were in a hurry (most of the time) the trailing E20 had the benefit of knowing what was coming toward it. Being passed at speed around bends by something large you knew was carrying a load, seemed to leave a lasting impression on people, so I can appreciate how the Datsun E20 service vans might have collected a certain 'mystique'.

Regarding one of our tandem E20 trips, Jamie said:

"... If u remember when we did the Melbourne to Brisbane trip in 15 hrs – towing the cars!

He [one of our team members] *refused to go home with me!"*

Waiting – always waiting for that sound…

Engines

LR18 – commonly referred to as the 'FIA'

The first engine I had any involvement with in the DRT was the single cam, nominally 1800cc motor which looked much like the standard production L18 motor used in 180B cars, among others. It has a specially cast competition cylinder head which strongly resembles a standard production L-series head but has enormous inlet ports and valves and round exhaust ports rather than the squarish-shaped ports on the standard head.

This engine as a package is externally most obviously distinguishable by the water manifold running the head's full length between valve cover and carburettors and incorporating a robust throttle linkage. The LR came with two twin-choke Solex Mikuni carburettors and stainless steel fabricated 4-2-1 exhaust extractors. It was always used wet-sumped as far as I know.

In my time, at least, it was homologated Group 2 and was used exclusively in the rally 610 SSS between 1972 and '74, and when Group 2 compliance was required in both the 710 SSS and the 160J Violet/Stanza in Australia between 1975 and '78.

There was also an LR20B version from 1978, which was based on the longer stroke version of the 4-cylinder, L series engine. These are identifiable by the extra, long 8mm dia. bolt, attaching timing cover to block at the top on both sides (the L20B block is 20mm taller.)

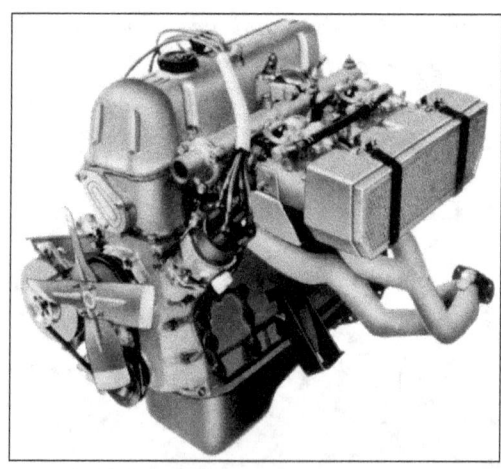

LZ18

The LZ engine in both 1.8 and 2.0 litre forms, together with the Z18ET from the Bluebird Turbo were the two engines I had most to do with in my time with Nissan.

The double overhead camshaft, 4-valve, LZ cylinder head sits atop an L-series cylinder block and it was initially developed in 1973 as the LZ14 to power the Sunny Excellents (KPB110) that ran in the Japan GP. Nissan entered nine of these in the '73 race and cleaned up, claiming the whole podium.

This was an L14 engine bored to 1598cc and could make 200PS at 9,400rpm. The special 16-valve cylinder head had a rather narrow, 34° valve angle and the engine ran with a compression ratio of 11.5 – 12:1 with flat top pistons, albeit with deep valve relief recesses. The camshafts were driven by a combination of gears from the crankshaft and a chain connecting the top gear and the camshafts (see photos).

The Nissan LZ cyl head from the exhaust side

Regulation changes meant that the LZ was mostly used for rallying from 1974 onward as the LZ18, winning the 1977 Southern Cross, and later the LZ20B, which dominated the Southern Cross from 1978 to '80. The LZ18 used an L18 block bored to 89mm to give 1941cc and made a nominal 200PS at 7,200rpm.

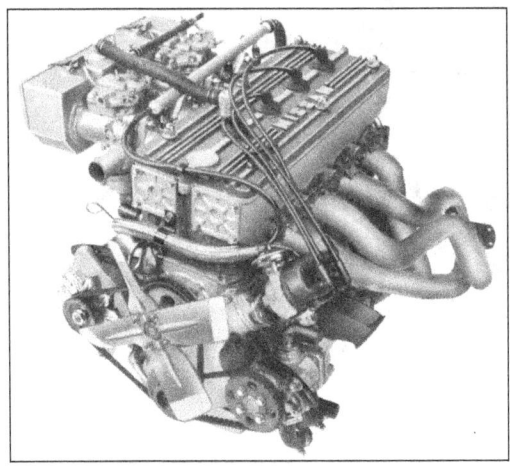

LZ20B

As far as I know, I was the first to adapt the LZ cylinder head and drive gear setup to an L20B short motor. I had new pistons made for the LR20 that came in our first Stanza and reassembled it with the head and cam drive set from one of the '77 Southern Cross motors.

The L20B block is 20mm taller than the L18 (allowing for the L20B's longer stroke) and my first challenge was to adapt the 10mm alloy plate holding the chain of seven gears, which take drive from the crankshaft up the front of the block. The holding plate bolted straight on, only requiring a small mod to enlarge an oil gallery hole. I then made up two pieces of 10mm aluminium, 20mm long and drilled for the extra timing cover retaining bolt, to extend the plate to the top of the block.

LZ cam drive gear plate (crank gear inset) and here covered and in situ. Les Collins photos

Rather surprisingly though, the major challenge was to procure a longer timing chain (the top timing gear is attached to a chain sprocket and this is chained to the camshaft sprockets, 20mm further away on the LZ20B. I tried everywhere I and my colleagues could think of but it turned out that the chain had been spec'd in metric measurements and Australia hadn't yet gone metric for roller chain. Online international purchasing was not yet a thing so I ended up solving the problem by sacrificing a second LZ chain, taking a few links from it to join to the first one.

In response to continued cam drive gear failure on the LZ engines, around the beginning of 1978 we had Peter Hollinger make a replacement for the sixth gear up from the crank, the one which usually failed.

These gears were straight cut and varied from around 40mm diameter to around 75mm. It was rather a complex system with the primary gear on the crankshaft being a single but gears two and three, four and five, and six and seven were pinned and welded together on common shafts, as was gear eight and the chain sprocket. The required backlash in six pairs of meshing gears (the spec. from memory, was a total of four crank degrees) was the cause of the characteristic rattle from the front of the LZ engine at low speed. Interestingly, when the LZ was used in racing, with longer duration cams, the engine did not produce the rattle. From this we deduced that the steepness of the cam lobe ramps, with the rally cams, was what caused the constant take-up of the backlash at slow speeds. This, plus the continual on-off the throttle in rallying, we felt was responsible for much of the stress and the cause of teeth breaking.

Installing the Hollinger-made replacement gear mostly solved this frustrating random failure in Australian built LZ engines. Not so for those from Japan however as Rauno's just-off-the-boat Stanza engine failed with this malaise in the first transport of the Endrust Rally which he was using as a shake-down for the Southern Cross later in the year.

Taller engine just fitted under the strut brace

Other than the fragility of the camshaft drive gears these engines also suffered from fuel rejection (or stand-off) and I found this very disconcerting when I first observed it on the engine dyno. At high speed fuel would spray back out of the intake trumpets so you'd see a cloud of fuel mist that might extend for 300mm or so. It was apparent there were wave pulses coming backwards through the head!

LZ20B motor built for display in my bedroom!

Les Collins spent many many hours trying to resolve a particularly bad case of this on an engine he built in recent years for a replica car. This head had larger than standard valves and ports. He was only able to mostly resolve the issue by fairly drastically reducing their size.

Fortunately, with a rally engine, the rejected fuel was trapped by an air filter and it was therefore important to tune the engine with air filter/s fitted.

The engine I built for George's '79 Cross car had an Australian cast cylinder block with steel sleeves fitted which allowed it to be bored to 90mm, so 2188cc. It had a Jack Mayes fabricated 4-2-1 exhaust extractor with 50mm primaries and 56mm secondaries feeding into a 75mm exhaust system, and it used the longer duration 76° camshafts. It produced 232bhp at 7,600rpm. It won too!

When I reflect on the LZ's record in Southern Cross Rallies, it surprises me that the Japanese engines proved so unreliable – con-rod bolt failures in 1975, piston failures (I believe for Källström) in '76, broken con-rods for Aaltonen and Källström in 1978 – for, although we had more than our share of troubles with the cam drive gears in Australia, we never experienced even one of the catastrophic bottom end failures the Japanese imports suffered. The crankshaft, con-rods and bolts, and the pistons, all seemed top quality components, it was hard to see any of them breaking under rally conditions – standard components seemed to do the job for most Datsun competitors.

I note in Monty's story from the 1980 Southern Cross, where he talks about them discovering the engine that failed them in the last division, was found to have had loose centre main bearing bolts! Could some of this record of failures be due to assembly lapses? This is almost too much to believe of a works operation in Japan – the engineers who came to Australia always seemed so fastidious. Maybe they were simply the cream and the rest were left behind to assemble engines??

LZ18 engines: Barry Bray's 2-door Stanza Sports Sedan engine (cw Lucas mechanical fuel injection) lines up with near Japanese spec rally motor (48mm Webers substituted for Solex Mikuni carbs)

L20B

For 1981, particularly as we were no longer competing against works Ford Escort dirt racers, it was decided we could get away with running a more standard engine in the Stanzas. I built a standard headed L20B engine using an Australian cast cylinder block, modified local crankshaft, locally made forged pistons, Japanese steel connecting rods and modified locally cast cylinder heads with 48mm Weber carbs. I think from memory it made a little over 205bhp.

It proved a little harsh at around 6,000 rpm which we put down to the crankshaft being less counterweighted than the works units so I fitted the works 240Z harmonic balancer to the front of the crank (which can be seen in the photo below as well as the dry sump oil pump which I retained after the 1979 experience with the wet sump.)

Geoff Portman completely dominated the Australian Championship in '81 with this engine, winning four of the five events (Ross Dunkerton won the fifth and we also collected 4 second places and one third from 13 starts from the three cars we ran that year.)

1981: Much modified L20B engine ready for Geoff's Stanza

Z18ET

The story of the development of the turbocharged and fuel-injected Z18 910 Bluebird engine, the E14ET from the Pulsar Exa Turbo, and the FJ20ET for the DR30 Skyline is covered in my companion book, *Nissan Sport: Touring Car Racing in Australia, 1981–85*.

✸ ✸ ✸ ✸

I'd lastly like to thank the businesses and people who supported me with engine development and machining work over these years.

Firstly, Tom Sekeres (a countryman of George Fury) who introduced me to the engine dynamometer and the sensory overload of our engines running at full power, up close and personal. Jamie, Les Collins and I bought his business when Tom wanted to retire and, from then on, I no longer had to make a booking!

Another countryman contact of George's, Garbor (whose surname I once knew), had a machine shop in Moorabbin which mostly turned out plastic injection moulding dies. He turned his hand, equipment and considerable skills toward our purposes on multiple occasions.

Brian Berryman of Berryman Engines became my go-to man for engine component machining and Rick McQuaige did a superb job on our cylinder heads for the last few years.

Dave Thompson built two very nice wet sumps for us and was always ready to enthusiastically lend a hand.

Jack Mayes built at least three sets of sand-bent exhaust extractors.

John Patterson of Special Piston Services always made our pistons.

Thommo, building one of two wet sumps for '79

Early Datsun Rally Successes

The following record of Datsun successes between 1962 and 1975 is an amalgam of information from George Denner's book, *Introducing Datsun to Australia*' (sadly lacking crew names), Bruce Wilkinson's records, the Southern Cross Rally website, and Tom Snooks' very recent compilation, *'A History of The Australian Rally Championship 1968 to 1988'* which includes event story and full results.

N.B. Ross Dunkerton switched from VW into a Datsun 1600 in late 60s and began his amazing record of rally successes in the marque, so the 1968 and 1969 uncredited West Australian successes below will very likely be his.

Year	Event	Model	Crew	Result
1958	Mobilgas Rnd Aust Trial	Datsun 1000	Okuyama/Namba/Wilko	1st Class A
1962	BP Rally of S.E. Aust	Cedric 1900	Wilson/Wilkinson	2nd Cl. C
1964	BP Rally of S.E. Aust	Cedric 1900	Wilson/Wilkinson	2nd in Class C
1967	SCR	1000	Wilkinson/Inglis	1st Class A
	BP Rally of S.E. Aust	1000	Wilkinson/Inglis	1st & 4th Class A
	WA Safari	1000		1st O/R
	WA Hills Rally	1000		=1st O/R
	WAC.C. Rally	1000		1st Class, 4th O/R
	WA 1000 Rally	1000		1st Class, 4th O/R
	Geraldton Sunshine Trial	1000		1st Class, 3rd O/R
1968	Southern Cross Int'l Rally	1600	Wilkinson/Inglis	1st Class C, 12th O/R
	Tasmania Rally Champs	1600		1st O/R
	VW500 Winter Rally SA	1600		1st O/R team
	Morris 850 500 Rally of SA	1600		1st O/R team
	AVCC Aunger 400 Rally SA	1600		1st O/R
	Barossa Valley 300 Rally SA	1600		=1st O/R
	Doug Bray Trophy Trial SA	1600		=1st O/R

Year	Event	Class	Crew	Result
1968	BP 1000 Hills Rally SA	1600		=1st O/R team
	WMMC 300 Rally WA	1600		=1st O/R team
	BP Rally of S.E. Aust	1600	Wilkinson/Inglis	2nd Class, 6th O/R
1969	Southern Cross Int'l Rally	1000	Wilkinson/Inglis	1st Class G
	BP Rally of S.E. Aust	1000	Wilkinson/Inglis	2nd Class, 11th O/R
	Tasmanian Rally Champs	1600		1st O/R
	SA Rally Champs	1600		2nd O/R
	BP 1000 Hills Rally SA	1600		1st O/R
	Forest 500 Rally WA	1600		1st O/R
	Safari East-West Rally WA	1600		1st O/R
	Pathfinder Trial WA	1600		1st O/R
	Mountain Circuit Trial Tas.	1600		1st O/R
	NW Ampol Dealers Trial Tas.	1600		1st O/R
	Classic Rally, ARC, Vic	1600	Roxburgh/Haas	10th O/R
	Winter Trial ARC, SA	1600	Jenkin/Mortimer	3rd O/R
1970	Ampol Round Aust Trial	1600 SSS	Herrmann/Schuller	=1st O/R
	Ampol Round Aust Trial	1600		1st Novice
	Ampol Round Aust Trial	1000		1st Class A
	BP Rally of S.E. Aust	1000	Wilson/Bonhomme	1st Cl. A, 6th O/R
	Cambridge Toyota 500, SA	1600	McLeod/Lock	1st O/R
	Warana Rally ARC, Qld.	1600	Osbourne/Coote	7th O/R
	Southern Cross Int'l Rally	1600	Wilkinson/Inglis	1st Class I, 6th O/R
	Southern Cross Int'l Rally	1600	Mcleod/Mortimer	1st Class C
	Tasmanian Rally Champs	1600		1st O/R
	Shell Safari Tas.	1600		1st O/R
1971	Eureka Rally, ARC, Vic	1600	Stanley/Forsythe	8th O/R
	Bunbury Curran ARC, NSW.	1600	Mulligan/Trumpmanis	9th O/R

ADDENDUMS

Year	Event	Car	Crew	Result
1971	Bunbury Curran ARC, NSW.	1600	Lang/Gocentas	10th O/R
	Akademos Rally ARC, Vic	1600	Wardill/Hocking	2nd O/R
	Southern Cross Int'l Rally	1600	Lang/O'Cleary	5th O/R
	Southern Cross Int'l Rally	1600	Iwashita/Ishikawa	6th O/R
1972	Bunbury Curran ARC, NSW	1600	Lang/O'Cleary	5th O/R
	Bunbury Curran ARC, NSW	1600	Elliot/Gocentas	8th O/R
	Snowy Mountains Rally ARC	1600	Lang/O'Cleary	6th O/R
	Snowy Mountains Rally ARC	1600	Jackson/Godden	10th O/R
	Alpine Rally ARC, Vic	1600 SSS	Goetz/Mitchell	=6th O/R
	Southern Cross Int'l Rally	240Z	Aaltonen/Halloran	2nd O/R
	Southern Cross Int'l Rally	180B SSS	Herrmann/Mitchell	4th O/R
	Southern Cross Int'l Rally	1600	Jackson/Godden	5th O/R
	Southern Cross Int'l Rally	1600	Goetz/McFadzean	10th O/R
1973	Southern 500 Rally ARC SA	240Z	Kilfoyle/Osborne	6th O/R
	Bunbury Curran ARC, NSW	240Z	Kilfoyle/Osborne	=2nd O/R
	Warana Rally ARC, Qld.	240Z	Evans/Lake	5th O/R
	Southern Cross Int'l Rally	180B SSS	Kilfoyle/Osborne	6th O/R
	Southern Cross Int'l Rally	240Z	Watson/Beaumont	8th O/R
	Southern Cross Int'l Rally	1200	Evans/Mitchell	10th O/R
	BP Rally of SE Australia	1600	Chapman/Comerford	1st O/R
1974	Semperit Rally ARC, WA	260Z	McLeod/Mortimer	2nd O/R
	Semperit Rally ARC, WA	240Z	Dunkerton/Large	5th O/R
	Akademos Rally ARC, Vic	240Z	Dunkerton/Large	2nd O/R
	Akademos Rally ARC, Vic	260Z	McLeod/Mortimer	3rd O/R
	Akademos Rally ARC, Vic	120Y	Evans/Mitchell	5th O/R
	Bega Valley Rally ARC, NSW	260Z	McLeod/Mortimer	1st O/R
	Bega Valley Rally ARC, NSW	240Z	Dunkerton/Large	3rd O/R

Year	Rally	Car	Crew	Result
1974	Bega Valley Rally ARC, NSW	120Y	Evans/Mitchell	4th O/R
	Bega Valley Rally ARC, NSW	1600	Cheesman/Lockie	5th O/R
	Uniroyal 1000 Rally ARC, SA	240Z	Dunkerton/Large	3rd O/R
	Uniroyal 1000 Rally ARC, SA	120Y	Evans/Mitchell	5th O/R
	Uniroyal 1000 Rally ARC, SA	260Z	McLeod/Mortimer	6th O/R
	Warana Rally ARC, Qld.	260Z	McLeod/Mortimer	2nd O/R
	Warana Rally ARC, Qld.	120Y	Evans/Mitchell	4th O/R
	Warana Rally ARC, Qld.	1200	Coote/Marsden	5th O/R
	Bunbury Curran ARC, NSW	260Z	McLeod/Mortimer	2nd O/R
	Bunbury Curran ARC, NSW	120Y	Evans/Mitchell	3rd O/R
	Bunbury Curran ARC, NSW	180B	Pike/Carli	4th O/R
	Alpine Rally ARC, Vic	260Z	McLeod/Mortimer	1st O/R
	Alpine Rally ARC, Vic	180B	Pike/Carli	6th O/R
	Southern Cross Int'l Rally	180B SSS	Fury/Suffern	4th O/R
	Southern Cross Int'l Rally	710 SSS	Iwashita/Yasuoka	5th O/R
	Southern Cross Int'l Rally	1600	Munro/Harris	7th O/R
1975	Mazda House ARC, NSW	710 SSS	Fury/Bonhomme	1st O/R
	Mazda House ARC, NSW	260Z	Dunkerton/Large	=2nd O/R
	Mazda House ARC, NSW	260Z	McLeod/Mortimer	5th O/R
	Toms Tyres 1600 ARC, WA	260Z	Dunkerton/Large	1st O/R
	Toms Tyres 1600 ARC, WA	260Z	Edwards/Philip	2nd O/R
	Toms Tyres 1600 ARC, WA	260Z	McLeod/Mortimer	3rd O/R
	Toms Tyres 1600 ARC, WA	240Z	Stean/Matthews	6th O/R
	Akademos Rally ARC, Vic	260Z	Dunkerton/Large	=1st O/R
	Akademos Rally ARC, Vic	260Z	McLeod/Mortimer	=1st O/R
	Akademos Rally ARC, Vic	710 SSS	Fury/Suffern	3rd O/R
	Bega Valley Rally ARC, NSW	260Z	Dunkerton/Large	3rd O/R

1975	Warana Rally ARC, Qld.	260Z	Dunkerton/Large	1st O/R
	Warana Rally ARC, Qld.	260Z	McLeod/Mortimer	2nd O/R
	Walker Trophy Rally ARC, SA.	260Z	Dunkerton/Large	2nd O/R
	Walker Trophy Rally ARC, SA	260Z	McLeod/Mortimer	3rd O/R
	Walker Trophy Rally ARC, SA	260Z	Pike/Walmsley	4th O/R
	Alpine Rally ARC, Vic	260Z	McLeod/Mortimer	1st O/R
	Alpine Rally ARC, Vic	1600	Harrowfield/Boyd	5th O/R
	Southern Cross Int'l Rally	180B SSS	Carr/Gregson	3rd O/R

1600 SSS of Herman/Schuller =1st O/R in the 1970 Ampol Trial

Datsun 1000 Bill Evans and Mike Mitchell in the 1973 Classic Rally.

Datsun/Nissan model nomenclature

Nissan/Datsun model naming and designation is nothing if not confusing. For the time period covered by this book at least, suffice it to say that Datsun is a name owned by Nissan Motor Co., Japan, and which they used for passenger cars exported from Japan between 1958 and 1986. By 1986 the name Datsun had been phased out and all vehicles were subsequently known as Nissans. In Australia, Nissan firstly used the Stanza and then the Bluebird Turbo to promote its change of name. For the whole muddy story on Nissan nomenclature, search 'Datsun' at wikipedia.org

The name Skyline began as a model line owned by the Prince Motor Co. but was integrated into the Nissan line up when the two companies merged in 1966. Search 'Nissan Skyline' at Wikipedia to discover just how many different vehicles have been sold with the 'Skyline' name.

The following table shows the models predominantly used by Nissan for motorsport in Australia under the names Datsun Rally Team and Nissan Sport.

From	Australian name	But also known as:	Notes
1958	1000	210, Bluebird	the 2-series body
1967	1000	B10, Sunny	built on new 'B' series platform
1968	1600	P510, Bluebird	H510 used for L18 versions. Also available in SSS (twin carb etc.) spec.
1972	180B SSS	KP610, Bluebird	K designates 2-door, all 2-doors sold in Australia at least were SSS spec.
1972	240Z	S30, Fairlady Z	
1974	710	160J, KP710, Violet	Slightly shorter body than a 610 (180B) but a very similar spec.
1977	PB210	120Y, Sunny	'P' in this instance indicates an L series engine rather than the A series as sold in Australia
1978	Stanza	A10, PA10/11 160J, Violet, Datsun 510	So confusing – body and spec significantly dissimilar to 1600 (P510)

Year	Model	Code	Notes
1981	Bluebird	P910	Produced and sold in Australia with L20B carburettored engine and live rear axle but raced here with Z18E turbocharged and electronically injected engine and independent rear suspension spec.
1985	Skyline R30		2 litre turbocharged FJ20E engine used for competition in Australia but all Skylines of this era sold in Australia with L24 engine (straight 6 cyl.)

PROJECT ACKNOWLEDGEMENTS

I have had a lot of help with the writing of this book. It would have been a far inferior finished product without the initial inspiration of Jamie Drummond, the eloquent character descriptions from Richard Power, and the direction to relevant early texts from Bruce Wilkinson.

I've also had assistance with remembering including the supply of many photographs from John Bosua, Barry Nelson, Bill Evans, Dave Thompson, Peter Ryan, Graham Symons, Mike Mitchell, Justyn Snooks, George Smith, Peter Anderson, Barry Bray, Geoff Portman, Ken Cusack and Teddy Webber.

The following have not only helped with the above but have also provided me with stories in their own words and their generous agreement for me to reproduce them here: Tom Snooks, Roger Bonhomme, Peter Davis, Monty Suffern, Jeff Beaumont, Ross Dunkerton, Lachlan Maclean and Bob Watson.

Three people have not only provided me with all of the above but have also fastidiously proofread and fact checked various versions of my manuscript. Thank you so much Jeff Cameron, Simon Brown and Roger Bonhomme – if the book is well received you should all take great credit. If there are criticisms it will be me who should fall on his sword.

Lastly, it would be remiss of me to fail to thank my partner, Robyn who has almost endlessly indulged me while I laboured to get this done. Thank you Darling.

www.ingramcontent.com/pod-product-compliance
Lightning Source LLC
Chambersburg PA
CBHW072001290426
44109CB00018B/2099